YOU

ARE THE

TEAM

6 SIMPLE WAYS TEAMMATES
CAN GO FROM GOOD TO GREAT

MICHAEL G. ROGERS

ISBN-13:
978-1546770855
ISBN-10:
1546770852

www.YouAreTheTeamBook.com

www.MichaelGRogers.com

info@MichaelGRogers.com

To my wife, Terri and my eight children and their spouses Kristen (Nate), Michael, Scott (Kiera), Kelli (Kyle), Jeffrey, Adam, Jacob and Nathan who love and support me. And to David Fares, the best leader I ever worked for and who inspired me many years ago in the practice of leadership and teamwork.

Contents

Introduction

Great teams are made up of teammates.

A story is told of a man in a truck who had become lost while driving through the country. He reached down to grab his drink when suddenly he lost control of his truck and ran it into a ditch three-feet deep.

Unhurt, but stuck and in the middle of nowhere, he needed some help to get his truck out. He spotted an old farmhouse about a quarter of a mile away and walked there to ask for help.

An old farmer answered the door, and the man described his situation. The farmer told him he didn't do much farming anymore, so he didn't have a tractor that could pull him out. He did, however, know a way he could help. He then pointed to an old mule standing in a field about 10 feet away. "Andy can get you out of that ditch," he said.

The man looked at the old mule and then back at the farmer who kept repeating, "Yep, Andy can do it." The man figured he had no other choice but to put his faith in this old mule. So the farmer, the man, and Andy—the old mule—took the walk to the ditch.

When they got there, the farmer hooked up old Andy to the truck and then took the reins and shouted, "Pull Henry! Pull Bill! Pull James! Pull John! Pull Andy!" And with relative ease, the old mule pulled that truck right out of the ditch!

The man was speechless. Patting the mule, he thanked the farmer for his generous help and asked, "Why did you call all of those other names?"

With a smile, the farmer replied, "Old Andy is pretty close to being completely blind. As long as he believes he is part of a team, he can pull anything."

And it's true! As long as we believe we are part of a team, we can do anything! Being part of an effective team feels good, and just like Old Andy, we can accomplish more things together than we ever could alone. We are happier and more productive when we are a part of a great team.

But who and what makes a great team? It's YOU! YOU bring a unique set of gifts and talents that no one else on the team brings. YOU bring a unique set of perspectives that no one else has heard. YOU bring a unique history and group of experiences that no one else has lived. And only YOU can personally commit to using your uniqueness and talents to help drive your team to greatness. Without YOU as an individual and as a teammate, there is no team.

Is there an "I" in team? Maybe not literally, but figuratively, yes! And the "I" (you) has to become great before a team can become great. Until each member of the team (the "I" and the "You") is committed to excellence, teams will struggle to become excellent. **Great teams are made up of great teammates!**

You Are the Team is about the six virtues (the *6 B's*) every member of a team must strive to live in order to be great.

1. Be Selfless. The first of the *6 B's* is about putting other team members' needs ahead of your own. When you serve others, and put the team and your teammates ahead of everything else, you are being selfless and doing your part to help the team succeed. Selfless teammates are highly regarded by the rest of their team.

2. Be Trustworthy. Trust is the foundation of teamwork and is the second of the *B's*. It is also the foundation of a person's character. By being trustworthy, teammates improve collaboration and communication on their team. When you tell the truth, do what you say you will do, and engage in honest discussions with your teammates, you become a trusted member of your team. Trustworthy teammates are seen as having integrity and are well respected by their team.

3. Be Humble. The third *B* helps everyone on the team become better because humble teammates are focused on the betterment of the team, and not themselves. When you take accountability, learn from your mistakes, seek feedback, and feel gratitude, you are being a humble teammate. Humble team members are appreciated by their teammates.

4. Be Positive. Positive teams have greater energy to accomplish amazing things. By personally applying the fourth *B*, teammates are improving the energy on their team. When you refrain from negativity (including gossip), compliment others, and celebrate a teammates success, you are being a positive teammate. Teammates who are positive are seen as a light of bright contagious energy by their teammates.

5. Be Respectful. Respectful teammates improve team relationships by living the fifth *B*. By being respectful, team members increase the trust, unity, and connection between them and their teammates. When you extend kindness, seek to understand teammates, and demonstrate empathy, you are being a respectful teammate. Respectful teammates are well liked and esteemed by their team.

6. Be Great. Great teammates lead the way for others, and this is the sixth *B*. Focusing on being great is an opportunity for teammates to lead and motivate their teams to be better. When you get it done and then some, are aware of your team's vision and goals, bring solutions, take time to develop yourself, and inspire and lead members of your team, you are being a great teammate. Members of teams are inspired by their great teammates.

In the following chapters, we will go into greater detail with each of these *B's*. While your team's commitment to these *6 B's* is important to the success of your team, the only commitment you can do anything about is your own. If you want a team of selfless, trustworthy, humble, positive, respectful, and great teammates, then be selfless, trustworthy, humble, positive, respectful and great yourself. Don't wait for your leader or other teammates to make it happen. YOU make it happen.

Like an orchestra, the conductor can only do so much if the musicians aren't committed to practicing. Your leader can only do so much as well if you and your teammates aren't personally committed to teamwork. But YOU can personally commit now that you will do your part.

YOU have the opportunity to bring something really special to your team! Your personal greatness can shine brightly for all who are on your team to see and follow. *You Are the Team* is about YOU. **Look at this book as an opportunity to make your team great by making YOU greater.** Not only will you become a more committed teammate but you will also find yourself becoming a better spouse, sibling, parent, and/or friend as well. That's because the principles we discuss in this book are universally applicable to all relationships. I invite you to discover with me how these powerful virtues can change your life.

Note: At the end of each section/principle is a question or two to aid you in applying what you learn. It would be worth your time to carefully reflect on each question.

Additionally, you will find a self-assessment at the end of the book. Please take the time to assess yourself as a teammate.

You can also find a more detailed application of the principles found in this book with additional questions and exercises in a separate and conveniently bound workbook at
http://www.michaelgrogers.com/books

YOU ARE THE TEAM

1. Be Selfless

At the heart of a successful team, you will find the selfless and caring hearts of its members.

The Civil War was one of the most bloody and vicious wars in American history. At least 620,000 men lost their lives in battle, which "accounted for approximately 2.5 percent of the entire population of the country at the time."[1] Total casualties exceeded those of all other American wars, "from the Revolution through Vietnam."[2]

In the winter of 1862, the forces of the Confederate Army's General Robert E. Lee were making progress in several key battlefields in the Eastern Campaign, including a victory in a heavily one-sided and bloody conflict in Virginia called the Battle of Fredericksburg. This was one of the most decisive yet detrimental conflicts the Union army had experienced in the Civil War. When U.S. President Abraham Lincoln got word of the Union Army's casualties in Fredericksburg, where one in ten Union soldiers had died, he cried, "If there is a worse place than hell, I am in it."[3]

The campaign in Fredericksburg had initially looked promising for the Union Army, but it quickly turned bad after bureaucratic delays and blunderings. On December 13, 1862, Union forces attacked the

Confederates at Marye's Heights, a large sloping hill overlooking the town of Fredericksburg. The Confederate army had fortified themselves against a stone wall that ran along the crest of the hill, sitting four deep and out of the sight of the Union army.

As the Union army began their advance, they were viciously ambushed by the hiding Confederates. By the morning of December 14, over 12,000 Union soldiers had fallen at the hands of the Confederate army; few Union soldiers came within 50 yards of their firing enemies.[4]

Many of those remaining on the battlefield were still alive, but they suffered from wounds, cold, and thirst. During that long night, both sides were forced to listen to the cries and moans of those soldiers still living, for hours. Several described these cries to be "weird, unearthly, terrible to hear and bear". Listening to these men who were "lying crippled on a hillside so many miles from home - broke the hearts of soldiers on both sides of the battlefield."[5]

Richard Rowland Kirkland, a 19-year old infantry sergeant for the Confederacy, could not bear to listen to the suffering soldiers any longer. On the morning of December 14, he asked his commanding officer if he could scale the wall and provide water for the suffering Union troops who could be seen. The young sergeant exclaimed to his commanding officer, "All night and all day I have heard those poor people crying for water. Water! Water! And I can't stand it any longer. I come to ask permission to go and give them water."[6]

The commanding officer initially denied Kirkland's request because of the danger, but later granted his permission. With several canteens hung around his neck and to the astonishment of men on both sides, Richard climbed the wall to provide much needed help. Several shots were instantly fired, thinking that Kirkland's motives were to wound more. However, after realizing what was happening, the shooting quickly ceased.

Sergeant Kirkland made his way to each soldier, comforting them the best he could by laying his jacket over one and providing water to the thirsty lips of another. For the next hour and a half, he would scale the wall a number of times with his canteens to get more water for his enemy as cries of "Water, water, for God's sake water" could be heard all over the field.[7] It was a heartfelt and loving act of service that stopped a vicious war for just a moment.

Sergeant Kirkland was a selfless hero who risked his life to aid an enemy that he had risked his life to defeat just the day before. It is safe to say that you most likely won't ever be asked to risk your life for a teammate, let alone a member of an opposing team, but you will have many opportunities to selflessly put the needs of others ahead of your own, just as Richard Kirkland did. At the heart of a successful team, you will find the selfless and caring hearts of its members.

Becoming a successful team begins with teammates who want to provide more value than they receive, who willingly and actively serve each other, who think of others first and put their own needs last, and who desire the success of the team over their own. As team members think of others first, they actually lose little and gain much more, as the following story illustrates:

"Two brothers worked together on the family farm. One was married and had a large family. The other was single. At the day's end, the brothers shared everything equally, produce and profit.

"Then one day the single brother said to himself, 'It's not right that we should share equally the produce and the profit. I'm alone and my needs are simple.' So each night he took a sack of grain from his bin and crept across the field between their houses, dumping it into his brother's bin.

"Meanwhile, the married brother said to himself, 'It's not right that we should share the produce and the profit equally. After all, I'm married and I have my wife to look after me and my children for years to come. My brother has no one, and no one to take care of his future.' So each night he, too, took a sack of grain and dumped it into his single brother's bin.

"Both men were puzzled for years because their supply of grain never dwindled. Then one dark night, the two brothers bumped into each other. Slowly it dawned on the them what was happening. They dropped their sacks and embraced one another".[8]

Teamwork is a win-win when its members are thinking about each other first. The teammate who gives credit to others often becomes credible. The teammate who serves another often becomes especially liked. And the teammate who always thinks of others first becomes loved.

While my kids were growing up, I asked them if they wanted me to let them in on a secret to getting lots of friends. After rolling their eyes (which was often the response of Dad's frequent "wisdom"), I told them to put others first. I counseled them to find ways to serve and genuinely compliment others, to help their friends and teammates become better people, and to pray that they would have more love for others. It's a powerful idea!

There is a Chinese Proverb that states: "If you want happiness for an hour—take a nap. If you want happiness for a day—go fishing. If you want happiness for a month—get married. If you want happiness for a year—inherit a fortune. If you want happiness for a lifetime—help others."[9] Happiness on teams is found in the selfless thoughts and acts of each teammate.

Give Service

A giving heart is the best kind of heart.

A few years ago, I was having lunch with a friend who is an emergency physician at our local hospital. We sat comfortably in a quiet booth at our favorite Mexican restaurant, surrounded by sombreros, colorful Spanish art, and soft music while eating tortilla chips and salsa. The perfect lunch!

I asked him a question that would completely change the way I thought about teams: What does teamwork look like in the Emergency Room? In response, he said it is about knowing the needs of each person on the team and how to assist and serve them. If the team is focused on one another's needs, they literally save lives.

At that time, I understood the concept of Servant Leadership, which consists of leaders who are servants first. Many religious leaders in world history have been servant-first leaders, including Jesus, Muhammad, Buddha, and modern leaders such as Mother Teresa. But from the moment my friend shared his answer, I began to also think about **Servant Teamwork**.

Many of us like to serve others in our homes, churches, and even communities, but rarely do we see that same level of service in our teams. However, when team members focus on each other's needs, great things happen as everyone works together. When teammates truly become servants to one another, the level of caring and trust on teams increases dramatically. I call it the "Service Effect."

This positive effect occurs when people begin to serve others. As they serve, they start to love and care more about those they are serving. And as their feelings of love and caring increase, their desire to serve more increases as well. ***Serve more, love more. Love more, and desire to serve more.*** What a great foundation and pattern for teamwork and—more importantly—life!

Parents are a prime example of this love and service pattern. From birth, a baby is totally dependent on his or her parents. The baby does nothing but eat, sleep, spit up, and mess diapers while parents tirelessly feed the baby, get very little sleep, clean spit up, and change lots of diapers. The parents' love for their baby increases and deepens, despite the baby's many needs. The love and service concept doesn't stop there, however. As the parents continue to nurture and take care of their little infant, the baby's love for his or her parents grows deeper as well.

Have you ever had a teammate do something nice for you? How did you feel about that person? If you are like most people, you never forgot the nice deed, and the "likability" of that person increased. After the kind deed, you most likely felt different about that person each time you saw them.

Years ago, our family moved several states away to a place where we knew no one. I had rented two of the largest U-Haul trucks you could get and packed them to the roof with our things. My two young teenage boys and my father (who had a bad back) were my only help to unload these two big trucks.

On a very warm July day, we pulled up to the driveway of our new home. We were exhausted due to the long drive and very little sleep. We did not look forward to the task ahead. Then, out of nowhere, eight men from the neighborhood showed up and helped us unload our two huge trucks. In about an hour or two, we were all moved in! Years later, I remember every one of those men and still get warm feelings every time I see them and think of their service to me and my family that day.

Again, when we do something nice for someone else, it completely changes how we feel about that person and how they feel about us. Can you imagine if every member of the team was actively looking for ways to serve each other, just as our neighbors took the initiative to help us move? How would that improve your team?

As you serve others on your team, you can make amazing things happen not only in your team but also in your personal life. Mahatma Gandhi once said, "The best way to find yourself is to lose yourself in the service of others."[10] Serving others is a great prescription for when you are feeling down or are in a bad mood. Next time you find yourself in such a state, do something nice for someone else, like a teammate. Your energy and attitude will begin to change as you lose yourself in the service of another. As Mark Twain once said, "The best way to cheer yourself up is to try to cheer somebody else up."[11]

Over the years, researchers have studied the correlation between service and happiness. Their results have shown that people who are altruistic are happier at work and less likely to quit their jobs than those who don't help others.[12] Those reasons alone should get you looking for opportunities to serve others more, right?

When teammates are looking to serve each other, the best and most welcomed questions they can ask are, "What can I do to better serve you?" "What can I do to ease your burden?" or "What can I help you with?" As soon as one teammate starts to take the lead in asking these types of questions to their fellow team members, there is a good chance others will begin to do the same. When somebody does something nice for us, most of us want to do the same. It's contagious.

In addition to the above questions, here are a few simple service ideas to get you started:

- Send a nice handwritten note of appreciation or recognition. Tell someone how their actions make your job easier. An email note is nice, but a handwritten note is personal.

- Volunteer to help with a project.

- Bring donuts, a dozen cookies, or any other dessert in for a teammate or the whole team. Next time you are making a dessert, make a double batch! Sugar is associated with sweet feelings.

- Make a list of teammates birthdays and personally recognize each of them on their special day.

- Take time to get to know your teammates and what they do outside of work. Ask how their son did in his last game, how their daughter did at her recital, or simply how their ski

13

weekend was. Teammates will feel like you personally care about them through these simple, thoughtful questions.

- Send a meaningful and unique gift to a teammate. Send something that reminds you of them and makes them feel special.

You will find that most of the principles taught in this book are focused on service, which is why it is discussed in the first chapter. Serving one another is the foundation and first step towards teamwork and developing all of the good feelings that are associated with being a team.

Application: Is there someone on your team you can serve right now? Why would serving them make a difference on your team?

Live the Platinum Rule

Truly try to understand what others want, not what you think they want.

All through our lives, we have been taught to adhere to the Golden Rule: Do unto others as you would have them do unto you. It is an old and time-tested rule that still has a great deal of application today. Many of us teach it to our children when we remind them not to hit their sibling because they wouldn't want their sibling hitting them.

But while the Golden Rule does put others first, it can fall short. For example, just because *I* like flowers as a gift, that doesn't mean *you* like them. Just because *I* like lots of detail when communicating with others, doesn't mean *you* do. Or, just because *I* prefer instant communication (e.g., IM, Text, Chat…) doesn't mean *you* do.

A good example that demonstrates the different types of problems the Golden Rule can cause is illustrated in the following story I once heard of a less-than-sensitive dad: Upon coming home from work one day, the father greeted his distraught wife. She relayed to him the sad news that their daughter's hamster had passed away and that she had been crying in her room for most of the day. The father thought it was an easy solution and went to his daughter's room to share that it was not that big of a deal and that they could simply get a new hamster at the local pet store for $6.95! As you can imagine, the mother was not very happy with her husband.

In this story, the father was simply responding as he would like someone to respond to him (just like the Golden Rule says). To him, it was an easy and fixable solution. But of course, what the daughter needed wasn't another hamster; she needed a father who simply understood how she felt and could console her. Unfortunately, these types of misunderstandings are not uncommon in families or on teams.

Can you see where living completely by the Golden Rule could become a problem in relationships and why treating teammates the way you would want to be treated can sometimes cause issues? If you subscribe only to the Golden Rule, you are approaching every relationship from *your* perspective, assuming that everyone is just like you. It can—and often does—backfire.

Instead of always doing unto others as you would have them do unto you, it is wise to also live by another type of Rule: The Platinum Rule. This states, "Do unto others as *they* want to be done unto."[13] The Platinum Rule is an "others first" rule; it is a selfless rule.

Let's use our previous Golden Rule examples and switch to using the Platinum Rule. Instead of getting flowers for a teammate, stop and think, "Is that something they really like? Are flowers a gift that would make them really happy?" Instead of including every single detail when talking to your teammate, stop and ask, "Do they really want to hear all of this?" Instead of insisting on communicating with instant messaging, instead ask, "What do I know about my teammate's communication preferences? Would they rather that I pick up the phone and call?"

People are too unique to live by the Golden Rule. No one sees the world the same way you do, and when we think that they do, we come up short more often than not.

I learned the value of the Platinum Rule through one of my earliest leadership roles: being a parent. With my first two children, I parented both of them the way I believed all kids should be raised. I gave consistent discipline, rarely raised my voice, and provided lots of love and hugs. I had read a number of books on parenting, and that's what most of the experts suggested. My first two children were pleasers, and it took little discipline to get them to behave. With these two kids, it felt like my parenting style was working, and I believed I could now write my own best seller on parenting!

Then came child number three. He was stubborn and didn't really care much about pleasing anyone, let alone his parents. I tried to raise him the same way I had the other two, but I wasn't as successful. The harder I tried, the more stubborn he became. I quickly learned that I would have to take a very different approach to raising him than I did with the other two and that it would require a great deal of patience as well!

The books I read in my early days of parenting didn't recognize that different kids would require different parenting styles. But I quickly did. Just like raising children, we can't afford to take a cookie-cutter approach to our relationships; we are all too different. It is important that you take the time to truly try to understand what others want, not what you think they want.

When you try to understand your teammates, you build stronger relationships on your team. Have you ever thought, "Wow, that person really gets me"? Odds are that person gets you because they are living the Platinum Rule, which requires you to regularly think about others first and put your teammates' needs ahead of your own. It is a powerful concept once you figure out what each teammate's needs are. How can you do that? Here are three ways to start:

1. Ask. Asking is probably the most obvious way to start learning what your teammates' needs and wants are. Just as leaders set time aside for one-on-ones, teammates can and should do the same. Once a quarter, or bi-annually, set aside 10 to 15 minutes with each member of your team. Ask them how you are doing as a teammate. Ask them what you can do to serve them more effectively.

Teammate one-on-ones are powerful, and they not only improve your practice of The Platinum Rule but also strengthen your team relationships and significantly increase trust.

2. Watch. Look for what people get excited about and what makes them irritable or angry. We can learn a lot by watching how others respond to us and to others. Meetings are a great place to observe teammates' likes and dislikes.

3. Do. As you start living the Platinum Rule, carefully pay attention to when you are successful and when you aren't. The application of the rule is where you learn the most about what others need; listen and observe carefully.

Application: Do you know what the needs and wants of your teammates are? How can you start putting others needs ahead of your own?

Put the Team First

Members of great teams are focused on achieving greatness together.

If you are putting others first, there is a good chance you are putting the team first. However, when egos, aspirations, politics, money, and gossip come first, they can quickly erode a team and its ability to achieve teamwork.

This is most recognizable on sports teams where an individual's ego and selfishness trumps the team's goal to succeed. This is the player who gets upset that he didn't score more, even though his team got the victory; the teammate who is highly critical of other teammates in an attempt to hide her own mistakes and weaknesses; the star player who frequently misses practice; or the teammate who refuses to give credit to the team and instead takes it for himself.

In their book, *Help the Helper: Building a Culture of Extreme Teamwork*, Kevin Pritchard and John Eliot quoted NFL football star Jerry Rice when asked on the ESPN show "Audibles" whether he thought the recent success of the Denver Broncos was the result of that team's quarterback, Tim Tebow, or the defense. He said:

> *When* are we going to get past the idea that one person or one thing is the reason for a group's success? Get over it all ready. It's killin' us. I think it's a big reason why our economy is struggling and why we don't have nonpartisan teamwork in Washington. The Broncos aren't winning because of Tebow or because of the D [defense]. They're winning because all fifty-three players and the coaches and front office and maintenance guys and ticket takers are pulling together, doing their jobs well. *That question's awful.*[14]

For any one person on a team to believe that they are more important or better than the rest of the team is presumptuous and naive. I have always loved the quote by Japanese writer Ryunosuke Satoro who said, "Individually, we are one drop. Together, we are an ocean."[15] We are so much more powerful together than any one of us is alone. However, putting personal egos aside and focusing on the team as a whole means teammates must be humble.

The All Blacks, a rugby team from New Zealand, are statistically the most successful professional sports team ever. They have won multiple championships in a sport where teamwork is everything. In 2004, however, things weren't so great. The team was losing, senior members of the team were threatening to leave, and discipline and

18

putting the team first were at an all-time low. The team needed a change, and new coach Graham Henry began the rebuilding process.

The team's new mantra became, "Better People Make Better All Blacks." It was believed that humility and other core principles were critical to the team's success. As they continued to rebuild their team, one of their foundations for future success became "Sweep the Shed." The players believed in leaving every locker room better than how they found it, whether home or away. This meant that even senior team leaders would be required to pick up trash or pick up a broom and sweep. It would also require that they leave egos at the door and live the team value of humility by example.

Could you imagine famous professional athletes in any other sport picking up a broom and sweeping the locker room? Putting the team first requires the humble efforts of every member (we will talk more about humility in the next chapter). When each member of a team puts their own egos and aspirations ahead of others, it can have dire consequences, just as the following old Indian fable of a Washer-man (a man who washes other's clothes for hire) and two donkeys illustrates:

The Washer-man had raised the two donkeys. He called one Donkey-A and the other Donkey-B. Donkey-A felt he was more energetic and could do better than the other donkey. He always tried to get the Washer-man's attention by taking more of the load and walking as fast as he could in front of his master.

Donkey-B was just a normal donkey. He tried as hard as he could, but he couldn't carry as much as Donkey-A or impress the Washer-man by walking in front of him. After a period of time, the Washer-man began to put pressure on Donkey-B to work harder, but Donkey-B couldn't meet his expectations. Eventually, Donkey-B started getting punished.

One day, Donkey-B was crying and asked Donkey-A to help. He said, "Dear friend, it is only the two of us. Why do we compete against each other? If we worked together, we could carry an equal load at a normal speed."

Donkey-A ignored the request and became even more competitive. The next day, he boasted to the Washer-man that he could carry more and run faster than Donkey-B, and he did. The Washer-man, as expected, became even angrier and demanded Donkey-B to go even faster, punishing him more when he couldn't! Suffering under immense pressure, Donkey-B collapsed in great fatigue and quietly passed away.

As a result of the collapse, Donkey-A felt like he was on top of the world, having proved his superior skills and abilities. But now he also had to carry Donkey-B's load. For a short time, Donkey-A was able to carry both loads, but he eventually became fatigued and weak. The Washer-man had no compassion on this once-superior but now tired donkey. He yelled and demanded more, but as hard as this donkey tried, he couldn't come close to satisfying his demands.

Finally, the day came when the Washer-man was tired of this fatigued and no-good donkey. He killed the donkey and went searching for some replacements. If only donkey-A had agreed to work together as Donkey-B had suggested, they would have both succeeded![16]

Teammates who put the team first are regularly thinking about the team's performance and how to be successful together. They realize they can't be as successful alone. No one is satisfied until everyone on the team is succeeding. They work together and take very little credit, preferring to give it to the team instead. Members of great teams discover that in order for one to succeed, all have to succeed. In the words of United States President Harry Truman, "It is amazing what you can accomplish if you do not care who gets the credit."[17] The best teammates use the word "we" more often than "I."

Bill Russell, an NBA Hall of Fame basketball player, once said, "The most important measure of how good a game I played was how much better I'd made my teammates play."[18]

While it is natural for team members to have some ego, possibly aspire to greater positions, and desire more money, great teammates don't let their individual desires override what is best for the team. These team members are focused on achieving greatness together, realizing that there is something bigger and better than themselves.

Application: How have you demonstrated recently that you are putting the team first? What are you specifically doing to help your team? What are you doing that hurts the team? What might you do differently?

YOU ARE THE TEAM

2. Be Trustworthy

Trust can take years to build, but it can be destroyed in a matter of minutes.

One of the tremendous wonders of the world is the Great Wall of China. It stretches over 13,000 miles, winding up and down, east to west across the mountains, deserts, and grasslands of China. Built by multiple generations over a 2,000-year period, the purpose of the wall was to secure China from its enemies.[1] Unfortunately, it failed.

Chinese emperors spent years and great expenses to build the Wall; however, in just a few years, it was breached three times by the enemy. How, you ask? Not by force or by overpowering armies, but by bribery. It should have been impossible for the enemy to penetrate the thick walls that stood up to 45 feet tall. But what was thought to be impossible became possible, and easily so, through dishonest and untrustworthy gatekeepers.

It took several dynasties to build the Great Wall, but it took only a few years to invalidate its greatness, all because of the corruption of those inside who were commissioned to guard and protect it. We can assume that because of their loyalty, the bribed guards were at one time deeply trusted by their Emperors; however, that trust was destroyed the moment they sided with the enemy. Trust can take years to build, but it can be destroyed in a matter of minutes.

Many people like to think that their teammates see them as trustworthy. While this is an important attribute to have, *it is something that has to be earned.* Being trustworthy is as much about what you say as it is about what you don't say and whether you truly "walk the talk."

Trustworthy teammates have each other's backs. They don't let other teammates down. They are there for each other, even when things become hard. Imagine you are dangling precariously from the edge of a cliff, several hundred feet in the air. The only thing between you and a fatal fall is a rope with a teammate who is holding on tightly at the other end. Take a look around your team. Who would you trust the most to have your back and hold the rope with all of their strength and not let go? Why do you trust them so much? Most likely it is because they are honest, dependable, caring and would do everything in their power to not let go. They have proven their trustworthiness in the past.

As a young boy, I witnessed first-hand the consequences of letting go of the rope. I had been selected to be on a tug-of-war team in grade school that was part of a bigger Olympic-type of event. We had gathered around the blacktop playground and were put on fairly even teams with about 20 kids on each side. A large ship rope was placed in each of our hands, and when our teacher gave the signal, we all started pulling as hard as we could. My team was beginning to win as we worked together in unison. Suddenly, as we pulled with all of our might, the rope jerked back, and we fell to the ground. It became apparent that something had gone terribly wrong. The kids on the other team were holding out bloody hands, with many of them screaming and crying. It was a scene that I will never forget. It turned out that a few members of the other team had given up and let go of the rope. As soon as they let go, the force of our pulling yanked the rope right through the hands of those on the other team who were still holding tight to the rope.

Trusted teammates hold on to the rope no matter how tough it gets. They understand that letting go has dire consequences to the rest of the team. Ideally, you would trust every member of your team to hold tightly onto the rope.

Both your own trustworthiness and the team's trustworthiness are foundational to teamwork. Without this kind of trust, teams won't work together. If you are afraid a teammate will let go of the rope, you won't ever hand your teammate the rope, and you can't win if you and your teammates aren't holding the rope together.

As you demonstrate your own personal trustworthiness and hold onto the rope, you can benefit greatly. Some of those benefits include:

- Teammates are more willing to work with you.

- Team members will ask for and trust your opinion more often.

- You will be less stressed because you never have to cover up the truth.

- You will have improved and more meaningful team relationships.

- You will gain greater opportunities and have more doors open for greater growth and advancement.

Trustworthiness is about telling the truth; doing what you say you will do; and directly, honestly, boldly, and respectfully engaging with your teammates. Such teammates never let their team down; they never let go of the rope.

Tell the Truth

Telling the truth isn't always easy, but it is always right.

Unless you follow professional tennis, you may have never heard of Jack Sock. But after a match on January 5, 2016, you might have. More than just tennis fans came to know the American tennis player after an incredible show of sportsmanship in a match against Australian champion Lleyton Hewitt.

Sock was ahead the second set of the match. Hewitt was serving to Sock when the linesman called out his first service. Pointing to the Australian champion, Sock shocked the crowd and chair umpire when he said, "That was in if you want to challenge it."

Baffled, Hewitt stood in disbelief as Sock encouraged him to challenge it. Eventually, Hewitt did challenge the call and was awarded the point. Jack Sock went on to lose the match, but he won the hearts and respect of many by his honesty.[2]

In a world where lying and deception have become commonplace and, unfortunately, frequently acceptable, it is refreshing to hear a story like that of Jack Sock. Would you trust him on your team?

James E. Faust, an American religious leader once said, "Honesty is more than not lying. It is truth telling, truth speaking, truth living, and truth loving."[3]

Telling the truth isn't always easy, but it is always right. Consider the times throughout your life when you have been brave enough to tell the truth, even when it was hard. What about the times you chose to lie instead of being honest? What sort of a difference did it make in how you felt? What difference do you think it made to others? When you tell the truth to your teammates, you improve the trust on your team and strengthen the lines of communication; not being honest does the exact opposite, and teams are weakened.

Plus, those who lie and fail to tell the truth are eventually caught, a principle that is demonstrated in this clever but somewhat troubling interaction between a customer and baker:

One day, a woman calls into her local bakery, upset about an order she had received.

The baker answered the phone. "Hello, Pamela's bakery. How can I help you today?"

"I just picked up an order of your dozen super fudge brownies an hour ago, and they have nuts on them."

"Oh, I am sorry about that. However, it says here that's what you ordered.

"No, I don't think so!" said the upset customer. "I am allergic to nuts. Why would I order something I am allergic to?"

"Okay, what did you mean to order?"

"Super fudge brownies, without the nuts of course."

"Alright," said the baker, willing to cooperate with her customer. "We will get another dozen brownies out to you in the next hour. Just make sure to give us the other dozen when we get there, okay?"

"Sorry, I can't," said the customer.

"Why not?"

"I ate them already."

One way or another, dishonesty catches up!

In his 1977 book *I'm Sorry, I Didn't Mean To, and Other Lies We Love To Tell,* social psychologist Jerald Jellison provided a stunning figure. He said that humans are lied to as much as 200 times a day. In 2002, Jellison's finding was given further credence in a study conducted by Robert Feldman of the University of Massachusetts, who found that in a 10-minute conversation, people were told an average of two to three lies.[4]

Have you ever thought about why it is advantageous for you to always tell the truth and be honest with your teammates? What sort of benefits would that have for you personally? Here are four simple advantages:

1. You Improve Self Confidence. What do you have to hide? Nothing! Those who tell the truth can look themselves in the mirror every morning with an increased confidence.

2. You Are Happier. When most people lie, they are always fearful that they will be caught or discovered (which they oftentimes are). As a result, they end up spending a lot of energy covering for themselves, ultimately causing themselves a lot of stress. When you tell the truth, you don't have to worry about remembering what you said to whom. Telling the truth makes for a happier and less stressful life.

3. You Build a Better Reputation. People who tell the truth are looked at as people of integrity. Think about the most respected members on your team. Are they people of integrity? Most likely they are.

When you tell the truth, others trust you more because of your reputation. If a situation arises where a teammate, for example, is blaming you for something serious, more people are likely to believe you because you have consistently told the truth in the past. As I once heard it said, trust equals "consistent, persistent, and predictable actions" over time.[5]

4. You Encourage Others to be Honest. When you are honest, you are an example to your teammates. They will notice your honesty and want to do the same. Honesty can always start with you.

In addition to the effects that being honest can have on both yourself and others, it is also important to note that telling even a small white lie can have negative consequences. Researchers from the University

College London (UCL) found that telling small, self-serving lies desensitizes the negative emotions in our brains associated with fibbing. They found that, over time, little lies will lead to telling bigger lies because our response to lying begins to fade.[6]

Great teammates are completely transparent. They don't fudge, not even a little bit. They don't make results, for example, appear bigger than they are; they don't leave out errors, whether they are critical or not; and they don't tell false stories about a teammate. In short, they simply tell the truth. Even when being honest may not seem to be to their advantage, great teammates understand that it really is.

Application: Are you completely honest with your teammates? If you aren't as honest as you could be, why not? What do you need to do differently?

Do What You Say You Will Do

Team members depend on each other. To let a teammate down not only affects that teammate's reputation and credibility but also the team's reputation and credibility.

A promise is a promise, right?

Abraham Lincoln, the sixteenth president of the United States, was often affectionately called "Honest Abe." His wife, Mary Todd Lincoln, once wrote a friend, saying that "Mr. Lincoln… is almost monomaniac [or insane and obsessed] on the subject of honesty."[7]

The following story demonstrates this claim:

Lincoln was once traveling in a stagecoach with a military colonel from Kentucky. After they had traveled several miles, the colonel took a bottle of whiskey out of his pocket and said, "Mr. Lincoln, won't you take a drink with me?"

Mr. Lincoln replied, "No, Colonel, thank you. I never drink whiskey."
They continued their journey for many more miles and had a very nice
visit. Eventually, Lincoln's traveling companion reached into his
pocket and took out some of Kentucky's finest cigars. He said, "Now,
Mr. Lincoln, if you won't take a drink with me, won't you take a
smoke with me?"

Mr. Lincoln replied, "Now, Colonel, you are such a fine, agreeable
man to travel with; maybe I ought to take a smoke with you. But
before I do so, let me tell you a story, an experience I had when a boy.

"My mother called me to her bed one day when I was about nine. She
was sick—very sick—and she said to me, 'Abey, the doctor tells me I
am not going to get well. I want you to promise me before I go that
you will never use whiskey nor tobacco as long as you live.' I
promised my mother I never would. Up to this hour, Colonel, I have
kept that promise. Now would you advise me to break that promise to
my dear mother and take a smoke with you?"

The Colonel replied quietly, "No, Mr. Lincoln, I would not have you
do it for the world. It was one of the best promises you ever made. I
would give a thousand dollars today if I had made my mother a
promise like that and kept it, as you have done."[8]

Just as Abraham Lincoln kept the promise he had made to his mother,
being a great teammate requires that you do what you say you will do.
If you say you will get back to a member of your team with something,
and/or by a certain time, then it is important that you do it.

I, like you, have had people break their word to me over the years.
What happens when a member of your team doesn't do what they say
they will do? Trust and respect are lost. Next time they claim that they
will get back to you or do something for you, if you are like most
people, you won't believe them and will prepare as if they will break
their commitment. Great teams can't afford to function like this. On a
team where everyone is honoring their commitments, trust and

productivity will naturally increase. On teams where this isn't the case, trust and productivity diminish.

Can you imagine the skepticism of a teammate when another teammate continues to make promises he never keeps? What about the credibility of a team member who continues to underperform on tasks she is responsible for? More importantly, can you imagine the waning belief and confidence in yourself if you aren't doing what you say you will do? Abraham Lincoln certainly understood this.

Let's face it: team members depend on each other. To let a teammate down not only affects that teammate's reputation and credibility but also affects the entire team's reputation and credibility. Great teammates have developed a character of integrity and do what they say they will do. Be committed and be a promise keeper. You and your team depend on it.

Application: Do you always do what you say you will do? If not, why not, and what will you do to change that?

Directly, Honestly, Boldly, and Respectfully Engage with Teammates

Teams become successful when its members are willing to give difficult feedback, challenge each other, resolve differences, and boldly propose their own ideas.

Teams and team members become truly great when they honestly, boldly, respectfully, and directly provide feedback to their coworkers, and when they aren't afraid to engage in debate from a place of caring. These team members are well respected, greatly trusted and often seen as leaders.

YOU ARE THE TEAM

During an interview being shot for the 1996 PBS special *Triumph of the Nerds*, Steve Jobs tells the story of a widowed man in his eighties that lived up the street when Jobs was a young boy.

One day, the older man asked Jobs to meet him in his garage. He had something to show him. When Jobs arrived, the man pulled out an old rock tumbler that consisted of a motor and a coffee can with a little band between them. He then invited Jobs to the backyard where they collected some very regular, very ugly and very old rocks. They put the rocks in the coffee can with a little bit of liquid and some grit powder. The old man then closed the can, turned the motor on, and asked Jobs to come back the following day.

Steve Jobs remembered the can making a big racket as the stones went around and around in the can when he left the man's garage. He came back the next day, opened the can, and took out several amazingly beautiful and polished rocks. Jobs states, "The same common stones that had gone in, through rubbing against each other like this (clapping his hands), creating a little bit of friction, creating a little bit of noise, had come out these beautiful polished rocks." Teams, he said, are like these stones.

Jobs goes on to say, "It's that through the team, through that group of incredibly talented people bumping up against each other, having arguments, having fights sometimes, making some noise, and working together they polish each other and they polish the ideas, and what comes out are these really beautiful stones."[9]

Like the rocks, we can be fairly normal, ordinary, and even a bit rough on our own. But through the process of honest teamwork, a little friction, and being uncomfortable at times, we can end up in a very different state. Teams become successful when its members are willing to give difficult feedback, challenge each other, resolve differences, and boldly propose their own ideas. However, this is easier said than done for most team members.

A number of years ago, I was unwillingly caught in my own difficult and uncomfortable employee conflict with a woman we'll call Pat. Pat was an older, louder, and very big woman who was a bit intimidating (I once heard that, in a rage, she had torn the door off a bathroom stall). As a new employee to the department, I came to find Pat was a "wealth of knowledge" on the history, politics, processes, and policies of the department—mingled with a good dose of gossip.

I tried to steer away from any negativity and judgments about my team and the department in general because I was new to the job and maybe somewhat wise as to what would happen if I did. After a while, it was becoming clear that Pat didn't really care for me, possibly because I tried to avoid some of her negativity.

About six months into the job, she stopped talking to me all together. Something was obviously wrong. I went to my manager for counsel. His advice was to simply talk to her face-to-face and be truthful. He said that nothing would get resolved until we talked about it. While his counsel was good, I was a bit terrified; I hated conflict. However, I decided I would do as he counseled and talk to her.

Pat passed my cubicle one afternoon, and I asked her if we could meet in one of the conference rooms. She asked, "Why?"

I told her I had noticed she wasn't speaking to me anymore and that I would like to talk about it. Her response, coupled with almost a sprint to the conference room was, "You bet!"

And I thought, "Oh boy, what have I done?"

When we got into the conference room, she quickly outlined everything about me that bothered her, and I in turn did the same in regards to her. We had what I thought was a very honest, respectful, and healthy discussion regarding our differences.

When we were done, I said, "I feel a lot better, Pat. Thank you for taking the time to meet with me."

Her response to that was, "I don't feel any better. In fact, I am going to continue to be (insert a few choice words here) mad for the next few months!"

Wow! Obviously, she wasn't feeling as good about things as I was. That wasn't the response I expected. However, within a few days, she completely turned around. She was kind and considerate. Being honest with each other and giving her the opportunity to get what she was feeling off of her chest worked. It wasn't easy (like rocks in a tumbler), but it was worth it!

It is amazing what a little conflict can do to build healthier and more trustworthy relationships. But why are we sometimes fearful of engaging in such discussions with members of our teams, whether it's one-on-one or in meetings?

There are several reasons, but the main one stems from a fear of conflict. For many of us, we don't want to hurt someone's feelings; we, ourselves, don't want to be challenged; we don't want to be labeled a "trouble maker;" we worry about being uncomfortable; and so on and so forth.

But conflict doesn't need to be personal, and it is actually good on teams—just as it is in all relationships—as long as it is healthy (i.e. based on trust and focused on resolving issues). Patrick Lencioni, who wrote the bestselling book *The Five Dysfunctions of a Team*, states "all great relationships, the ones that last over time, require productive conflict in order to grow. This is true in marriage, parenthood, friendship, and certainly business."

He goes on to say, "Unfortunately, conflict is considered taboo in many situations, especially at work."[10] And it's true. Lencioni says people actually spend a lot of time and energy trying to avoid conflict. However, by engaging in directness, honesty, and healthy conflict from time to time, teammates can actually prevent the types of "back door politics" we unfortunately see too often.

34

Back door politics is when like-minded team members leave meetings and discuss the uncomfortable things that should have been brought up in the meeting. Teammates have these back-door discussions in closed offices, break rooms, and even parking lots. Lencioni calls this the "meeting after the meeting."

In these "meetings after the meeting," team members say things to each other like, "Can you believe Jim even proposed that idea?" Or, "If Jane would tweak this a little, the product could be so much better." Or, "I don't agree with the direction we are going?" Or, "Tim isn't pulling his weight on the project; it's not fair!"

Instead of honestly addressing these important issues in the meeting, team members are talking to others in vain and nothing is being solved or resolved. Teammates want to be heard, but when issues are addressed through back door politics, the right people (the team) aren't hearing it. Meetings become less efficient and even boring, gossip and negativity begin to spread quickly, team members don't buy into decisions, and the team ultimately fails to tap into the power of teamwork that it is capable of.

As a member of a team, you have an important responsibility to actively participate in meetings. You need to challenge and suggest ideas, provide direct and necessary feedback to teammates, resolve differences, and support and encourage members of your team. Just like the rocks discussed in Steve Jobs' story, your responsibility is to be fully committed to the team by bumping up against each other. Challenge each others' ideas when necessary, engage in passionate debate when needed, and work towards polishing the efforts of the entire team.

But participating in this level of commitment requires you to really care.

It takes courage to be honest and to challenge an idea, to call out a teammate or provide candid feedback. It is uncomfortable, for sure, but your honesty will pay huge dividends in the long run. As a result, your teammates will gain greater trust and respect for you because they know you care. Being a trustworthy teammate requires you to do so.

Application: How can you be more direct and honest in your engagements with teammates? What kind of positive impact would it have on your team and why?

3. Be Humble

Being a humble teammate takes time and great effort, and it isn't always comfortable.

"One afternoon in 1953, reporters and officials gathered at a Chicago railroad station to await the arrival of the 1952 Nobel Peace Prize winner. He stepped off of the train—a giant of a man, six-feet-four, with bushy hair and a large moustache.

"As cameras flashed, city officials approached with hands outstretched and began telling him how honored they were to meet him. He thanked them politely and then, looking over their heads, asked if he could be excused for a moment. He walked through the crowd with quick strides until he reached the side of an elderly black woman who was struggling as she tried to carry two large suitcases.

"He picked up the bags in his big hands and, smiling, escorted the woman to a bus. As he helped her aboard, he wished her a safe journey. Meanwhile, the crowd tagged along behind him. He turned to them and said, 'Sorry to have kept you waiting.'"

"The man was Dr. Albert Schweitzer, the famous missionary-doctor who had spent his life helping the poorest of the poor in Africa. A member of the reception committee said to one of the reporters: "That's the first time I ever saw a sermon walking."[1]

That day, the crowd was taught a great lesson in humility and service. Like Dr. Schweitzer, our own personal humility can change and inspire others. However, becoming a humble teammate takes time and great effort, and it isn't always comfortable. Humility is something we consciously develop; it is not something we simply wish for and have it magically become part of our character.

Humble teammates take personal accountability for team outcomes. They look at themselves and ask, "What could I have done better?" When expectations are not met; they don't blame others. Humble teammates also don't view mistakes as bad, but as an opportunity to learn and improve. They understand that making mistakes is part of the learning process.

When teammates are humble, they are consistently grateful for what others do for them. They regularly and gratefully consider how others affect their success. In addition, a humble teammate is genuinely happy for the success of their coworkers, not envious of it. They are confident enough in themselves and are not threatened by another's success.

Take Accountability

Taking accountability isn't always easy; however, it is the right thing for you, your team, and your organization.

On June 2, 2010, Armando Galarraga, a pitcher for the Major League Baseball Detroit Tigers, was one out from pitching a perfect game, something that is rare in Major League Baseball. Pitching a perfect game means that in at least nine innings, not a single opposing player gets on base. However, on the last out, the first base umpire, Jim Joyce, ruled the runner safe and put an end to Galarraga's quest for a perfect game.

Joyce believed that he made the right call; that is, until he saw the replay for himself after the game. The replay showed that the runner was clearly out and that Galarraga should have gotten credit for a perfect game. The humble umpire tearfully and immediately went to the 28-year-old pitcher from Venezuela and apologized for getting the call wrong.

What happened next is just as great! Galarraga turned around and forgave Joyce for blowing a call that cost him something he may never do in his career again: throw a perfect game. "He probably feels more bad than me," Galarraga said. "Nobody's perfect. Everybody's human. I understand. I give the guy a lot of credit for saying, 'I need to talk to you.' You don't see an umpire tell you that after a game. I gave him a hug."[2]

It is amazing how taking accountability for your actions can soften hearts, even in what seems to be the most serious of situations. Instead of denying his mistake or just simply shrugging his shoulders and saying, "That's the way the game goes," Jim Joyce stepped up in a big way and humbly took complete accountability for his wrong call.

Don't you love people like this? Jim Joyce demonstrated accountability, and both Joyce and Galarraga showed great humility in how they handled a difficult situation. Practicing accountability on successful teams means that each member is completely responsible for their own actions, as well as any consequences that may follow. Early in my career, I had the good fortune of being part of a team that taught me some valuable accountability lessons.

I had just been put on a brand-new team that was "testing the waters" with our fairly new leader. Our team was asked to travel to a meeting at one of our regional offices to discuss our new strategy for the coming year. The morning of the first day, a good portion of the group arrived later than 8:00 AM, the time we were told to be at the meeting. You could see our new boss becoming more and more frustrated as each latecomer arrived, poured a cup of coffee, buttered a bagel, and settled into their seat, oblivious to their tardiness.

Once everyone had settled, our new leader made his expectations around promptness very clear, though it should have already been clear by an email he had sent out the day before. During the next couple of days, not a single member of our team was late. My assumption is that most of the team didn't feel they had done anything wrong when they arrived late because others still hadn't arrived. But their assumption was wrong; it was faulty thinking.

Those who arrived late could have rebelled, rationalized their lateness, and even spoken badly about our new leader; fortunately for the team, they didn't. Each member of our new team clearly understood what they had done wrong and took accountability for it. Would it have been better if everyone had simply arrived on time in the first place, as they were instructed in the email the day before to do? Sure; that's how great teammates think. But what is important is that those who were late owned up to their mistake and didn't repeat it. In short, they became accountable.

In addition to owning up to mistakes and not repeating them, accountable teammates are proactive. They understand that each member of the team shares the responsibility for the goals and success of the team as a whole. Instead of waiting to be told to do something— or even worse, being told after the fact—they step up and take accountability for their actions. Accountable team members do things differently.

One powerful example of this is demonstrated in something that happens regularly on most teams: meetings. Instead of begrudgingly attending another "boring meeting," great teammates ask, "What am I accountable for in this meeting?" They also ask, "What level of involvement and engagement am I responsible for? How can I be better prepared for the meeting?"

Asking these questions is very different than simply moving through the motions of your responsibility to attend the meeting. It is another level of your personal accountability as a meeting participant and team member.

As you seek to take accountability on your team(s), don't try to place blame on others, make excuses for why you failed, or whine about expectations. Instead, ask what you could have done differently and look for what you will change in order to move forward and improve the team, goals, and results. Taking accountability isn't always easy, as demonstrated by the Umpire Jim Joyce; however, it is the right thing for you, your team, and your organization.

Application: What can you do to implement more personal accountability on your team and improve team goals and results?

Learn from Your Mistakes

The only mistakes that have any real negative consequences are the ones we fail to accept and learn from.

Jack Canfield and Mark Vincent Hansen tell the following wonderful account in their book, *A 2nd Helping of Chicken Soup for the Soul*:

"I recently heard a story from Stephen Glenn about a famous research scientist who had made several very important medical breakthroughs. He was being interviewed by a newspaper reporter who asked him why he thought he was able to be so much more creative than the average person. What set him so far apart from others?

"He responded that, in his opinion, it all came from an experience with his mother that occurred when he was about two years old. He had been trying to remove a bottle of milk from the refrigerator when he lost his grip on the slippery bottle and it fell, spilling its contents all over the kitchen floor—a veritable sea of milk!

"When his mother came into the kitchen, instead of yelling at him, giving him a lecture or punishing him, she said, 'Robert, what a great and wonderful mess you have made! I have rarely seen such a huge puddle of milk. Well, the damage has already been done. Would you like to get down and play in the milk for a few minutes before we clean it up?'

"Indeed, he did. After a few minutes, his mother said, 'You know, Robert, whenever you make a mess like this, eventually you have to clean it up and restore everything to its proper order. So, how would you like to do that? We could use a sponge, a towel, or a mop. Which do you prefer?' He chose the sponge and together they cleaned up the spilled milk.

"His mother then said, 'You know, what we have here is a failed experiment in how to effectively carry a big milk bottle with two tiny hands. Let's go out in the back yard and fill the bottle with water and see if you can discover a way to carry it without dropping it.' The little boy learned that if he grasped the bottle at the top near the lip with both hands, he could carry it without dropping it. What a wonderful lesson!

"This renowned scientist then remarked that it was at that moment that he knew he didn't need to be afraid to make mistakes. Instead, he learned that mistakes were just opportunities for learning something new, which is, after all, what scientific experiments are all about. Even if the experiment 'doesn't work,' we usually learn something valuable from it."[3]

On your team, you and others will make mistakes. Will you look at them as opportunities to learn and succeed, or as failure? Businessman Thomas Watson Jr. said, "If you want to increase your success rate, double your failure rate."[4] John Wooden, the legendary college basketball coach, once said, "The doer makes mistakes, mistakes come from doing, but so does success."[5]

A good way to see if you are on the right path is to ask yourself these questions: How do I react to my own mistakes and those of my teammates? Do I admit when I am wrong?

Trying to cover up your mistakes is not a good idea. It prevents problems from getting resolved, results in missed opportunities to learn, and wastes precious energy. It may even come to the point where teammates come to resent you, especially if you are looking to blame others and throw them under the bus.

Most of the things we learn in life are **not** free of errors. We are going to make mistakes, and we are going to be wrong on occasion. From the time we were babies, we learned how to do new and unfamiliar things by failing. Whether it was learning how to walk, how to sing the ABCs, or how to ride a bike, all of us made lots of mistakes.

If you are afraid to make mistakes, you are afraid to try new things. In short, if you aren't making mistakes, you aren't learning! Our reluctance to admit any type of weakness often comes from our inability to separate actions from our own self-identity. By admitting a mistake, we believe that others will see us as incapable or less intelligent. This is a terrifying thought for some people; however, none of it is true. When we admit our mistakes, we are often seen as more capable, intelligent and even more credible.

In the 1980's, there was a group of researchers at Cleveland State University that made an unexpected discovery:

In an experiment, these researchers created two fictitious job applicants, David and John. Both applicants had identical résumés and letters of recommendation; however, in John's letters, there was the sentence, "Sometimes, John can be difficult to get along with." Both résumés were shown to several Human Resources directors. Which applicant do you suppose the directors preferred? Surprisingly the majority of them chose difficult-to-get-along-with John.[6]

It was concluded that the criticism of John made the praise of him more believable. Admitting John's weaknesses actually helped sell him. In short, admitting your flaws gives you more credibility! The more you are willing to admit your mistakes and take full responsibility for your actions, the more believable you will be. Humbleness does pay, if you give it a chance.

Teammates who aren't afraid to admit their weaknesses from time to time are trusted more by their teammates. They are seen as being more caring about the team and its outcomes due to taking personal accountability for their own actions. In fact, they may even be seen more as leaders by their teammates, due to their humble nature and approach.

Everyone makes mistakes. ***Admit them, take accountability, apologize if necessary, and move on.*** Creating a culture of admitting, embracing, and learning from mistakes starts with you. Like many of the concepts in this book, it becomes contagious as you take the lead.

If a teammate makes a mistake, listen to them, accept their mistake, encourage them to do better, and move on. Remember, doing so is all part of becoming a great team. The only mistakes that have any real negative consequences are the ones we fail to accept and learn from.

Application: Think about a recent mistake you or a teammate made. How did you handle it? Why did you handle it that way? Is there anything you would do differently next time?

Seek Feedback

Getting feedback from your teammates is a gift to you from the team, and to the team from you.

Years ago, my wife and I were not seeing eye to eye, as married couples do on occasion. At the time, I was frustrated, so I blurted out, "Honey, just give me a list of five things I can do right now to be a better husband!" And she immediately went to work on the list.

When she was done with it, she quickly handed it to me. I am sure she thought that I wouldn't do anything with the list when, in fact, I actually did. I took that list with me wherever I went and really tried to improve. I had asked her for the list, and now it was my responsibility to follow through on what I committed to doing.

Fast forward several weeks later, and I am on a consulting trip in South Dakota. As I am unzipping my suitcase to unpack, I notice my list sitting on top of my clothes. I thought, *That's interesting; I didn't put the list there. I could have sworn I put it under my clothes.* As I picked up the list, I noticed that there were five more improvements added to the original five my wife had put down!

Be careful what you ask for, right? But all joking aside, when you ask for feedback on how you are doing, don't be surprised to find that people are willing to give it. And that is a good thing! People want to provide the feedback and you need the feedback. It is a bit cliché, but feedback is a gift. If I hadn't asked my wife, how would I have ever known how I could improve as a husband? Likewise, how could you ever improve as a team member without asking? Getting feedback from your teammates is a gift to you from the team, and to the team from you. Your teammates have the combination to unlocking personal performance barriers you aren't even aware of. All you have to do is ask.

Most companies do lots of customer surveys. Why? Because by getting feedback from customers, they are able to better understand where they are falling short and how they can improve. Likewise, getting feedback from your team helps you better understand your gaps and weaknesses and what you can do to become a better teammate, performer, and person.

Here are some specific ideas on how to get feedback. It may take some time to get quality responses, but eventually teammates are going to give more thoughtful feedback as they see you taking action to improve.

1. Ask. The first step to getting feedback from your teammates is to, of course, ask. You can ask with a survey, or ask face-to-face. I wouldn't recommend the survey be anonymous; doing so limits your ability to follow up and build trust with your teammates.

How you ask for feedback can make a difference in the responses you receive. Don't simply ask, "How am I doing?" This will only get you a one- or two-word response like, "Great!" "Pretty good." "Okay," etc. Instead, ask, "What are two or three specific things I can do to improve?" Or even better, "What are two or three things I do that hurt the team?" This latter question helps your teammate get even more specific. And don't only focus on the negatives. Be sure to ask, "Can you tell me two or three things I am doing really well?" Or, "Can you tell me two or three things I should keep doing?"

2. Listen. An important step in building trust when asking for feedback is to listen carefully. The natural reaction to getting feedback, especially if it hurts, is to become defensive and make excuses. Try not to take the feedback personally, but objectively. Remind yourself that the person giving you the feedback is taking a risk. They are giving you the feedback because they care, not because they don't like you or have some personal agenda against you. You asked for the feedback; your teammate trusts that you really want to receive it.

If you are receiving feedback face-to-face or over the phone, be careful not to interrupt with questions or excuses. Instead, be in the act of really listening.

3. Acknowledge. Once your teammate has given you feedback, acknowledge that you have heard it and that you genuinely appreciate it. It is important to say "thank you," and share not only what specifically you are going to do to improve but also that you look forward to becoming better. If you do have questions, ask them. But only ask questions to clarify, not with the purpose of defending yourself.

4. Act. Feedback doesn't do anybody any good if you don't act upon it. In fact, not acting on feedback erodes the trust others have in you. By asking for feedback, you are committing to doing what your teammates give in return. When you don't follow through on the tips you are given, it is the same as saying you are going to do something and not doing it—we already discussed the consequences of that in Chapter Two.

5. Follow Up. Once you start making improvements based on the feedback you have received, take time to thank those who gave you the feedback. Provide them with an update on your progress and ask them if they have noticed any improvement.

6. Repeat. Put a regular quarterly or bi-annual date on your calendar to get feedback and continue the cycle of asking, listening, acknowledging, doing, and following up.

Just like the other *B's* and corresponding principles we discuss in this book, asking for feedback is contagious. Once you start seeking feedback and seeing personal improvement because of it, others on the team will start to do the same. You will be better, and your team will be better.

Application: How are you at receiving feedback? Is it difficult for you? If yes, why? What can you specifically do to get regular feedback from your team in the future?

Show Gratitude

First comes gratitude, then a happy attitude!

Captain Charles Plumb was a US Naval Academy graduate and jet fighter pilot in Vietnam. He had flown a combined 75 successful combat missions when his plane was destroyed by a surface-to-air missile. Plumb ejected and parachuted down right into enemy hands, spending the next six years in a Vietnamese prison camp.

Plumb survived the experience and now spends his time speaking to audiences around the world about the lessons he learned. In his book, *I'm No Hero,* he shares the following story:

"Recently, I was sitting in a restaurant in Kansas City. A man about two tables away kept looking at me. I didn't recognize him. A few minutes into our meal he stood up, walked over to my table, looked down at me, pointed his finger in my face and said, 'You're Captain Plumb.'

"I looked up and I said, 'Yes sir, I'm Captain Plumb.'

"He said, 'You flew jet fighters in Vietnam. You were on the aircraft carrier *Kitty Hawk.* You were shot down. You parachuted into enemy hands and spent six years as a prisoner of war.'

"I said, 'How in the world did you know all that?'

"He replied, 'Because, I packed your parachute!'

"Well, for a guy who travels the world speaking, I was suddenly speechless! I staggered to my feet and held out a very grateful hand of thanks. This guy came up with just the proper words. He grabbed my hand; he pumped my arm and said, 'I guess it worked!'

"'Indeed it did, my friend', I said, 'and I must tell you, I've said many of prayers of thanks for your nimble fingers, but I never thought I'd have the opportunity to express my gratitude in person.'

"He said, 'Were all the panels there?'

"'Well,' I said, 'I must be honest—of the eighteen panels in that parachute, I had fifteen good ones. Three were torn, but it wasn't your fault, it was mine. I jumped out of that jet fighter at a high rate of speed, close to the ground. That's what tore the panels in the chute. It wasn't the way you packed it.'

"'Now let me ask you a question," I said, "do you keep track of all the parachutes you've packed?"

"'No,' he responded. 'It's enough gratification for me just to know that I've served.'

"I didn't get much sleep that night. I kept thinking about that man. I kept wondering what he might have looked like in a Navy uniform; bib in the back, bell-bottom trousers, a Dixie-cup hat. I wondered how many times I might have passed him on board the *Kitty Hawk*. I wondered how many times I might have seen him and not even said 'good morning', or 'how are you', or anything—because, you see, I was a fighter pilot and he was just a lowly sailor. But again, how many hours must that sailor have spent at that long wooden table in the bowels of that ship weaving the shrouds and folding the silks of those life-saving parachutes? I'm ashamed to admit that at the time, I could have cared less… until one day my parachute came along and he packed it for me!"[7]

Who on your team and/or in your organization is packing your parachute? Who is making your life easier? Have you felt or expressed your gratitude lately?

Have you been grateful and thanked your team's administrative assistant, for example, who sets up the spread of snacks and drinks for your all-day meeting? Or do you simply think, "Nice snacks"? Are you thankful to your I.T. team, who ensures that you have a functioning computer and the right software? Do you tell them you are grateful, or do you simply think, "That's what they get paid to do"? Are you focusing on being grateful and thanking a teammate for fulfilling a unique role and contribution on the team with their knowledge, skills, talent, or time? Or do you simply think, "I have my job to focus on, and they have theirs"?

YOU ARE THE TEAM

Every one of us has someone who helps us make it through the day, who makes us and the team better. Being grateful and expressing it feels good—it feels good to you, to a teammate, and to the entire team. A lot of energy can be created when a team is feeling and expressing gratitude for and to each other.

In addition to feeling good and blessing others, there are other tangible benefits to being grateful as well. Research shows that our health is better when we are more thankful. Our immune system is stronger, we are bothered less by aches and pains, we sleep longer, and we have higher levels of positive emotions. Our relationships are better because we are happier when we are grateful, and people prefer to be around happy people. Personal productivity also improves due to greater passion and commitment levels.[8] Thus, teammates are more inspired and productive when they know others are grateful for what they do.

Take some time to reflect on what you are grateful for? Are you thanking members of your team for "packing your parachute?" Are you working hard to carefully pack theirs? If not, there is never a better time to start then now.

Application: Who can you thank today for "packing your parachute"? What kind of impact would it have on them and why?

4. Be Positive

Positive energy on teams starts with one positive teammate—let that positive teammate be you!

In a remote Japanese village, there was a happy and energetic little puppy that heard of a place called "The Palace of 1,000 Mirrors" and decided to pay a visit. When he arrived, he playfully bounced up the steep stairs to the open door of the house. He entered the palace with his ears perked and his tail wagging very fast. To his surprise, this little puppy found 1,000 other happy puppies just like him, all of who were also wagging their tails just as he was.

He gave a great big smile and found the other 1,000 dogs smiling right back, which made him smile even bigger. The bigger he smiled and the faster he wagged his tail, the more the other 1,000 puppies smiled and wagged their tails.

As he left the palace, he said to himself, "What a wonderful place! I must come back and visit again."

In the same village, there was an older and very grumpy dog. He also decided to visit the palace of 1,000 mirrors. As he approached the door with his sad head hung low, he looked up and found 1,000 other

51

grumpy and unhappy dogs staring back at him. He growled and was frightened by the other dogs growling at him. He quickly left and said to himself, "That place is dreadful and a bit terrifying. I won't ever go back again."[1]

Your attitude as a teammate is important to your team's success. If you are always frowning and spreading negativity, you will most likely get frowns and negativity back. If you rarely take the time to see the good in others, very few will see the good in you. And if you don't take the time to compliment others, you will rarely get a compliment in return.

What you give to the team is reflected back to you. Each of us visits the Palace of 1,000 Mirrors every day; how you present yourself to each mirror is your choice. Even if most of your team is looking in the mirror with a frown, you can choose to look at the mirror with a smile and make a positive difference. Choosing to lead with a positive attitude helps you become the kind of teammate that makes great things happen on your team!

Be the change you want to see. In other words, be positive about your relationships with teammates, the team's goals, and your team's outcomes, and always look for ways to celebrate successes. The philosopher and psychologist William James once said, "Pessimism leads to weakness, optimism to power."[2] Imagine the power of a team full of optimists! Positive energy on teams starts with one positive teammate —let that positive teammate be you!

Refrain from Negativity

Positive teammates contagiously create positive teams.

Globally renowned leadership author and expert John Maxwell tells the following funny story:

"Fred and Martha were driving home after a church service. 'Fred,' Martha asked, 'did you notice that the pastor's sermon was kind of weak today?'

"'No, not really,' answered Fred.

"'Well, did you hear that the choir was flat?'

"'No, I didn't,' he responded.

"'Well, you certainly must have noticed that young couple and their children right in front of us, with all the noise and commotion they made the whole service!'

"'I'm sorry, dear, but no, I didn't.'

"Finally in disgust Martha said, 'Honestly, Fred, I don't know why you even bother to go to church.'"[3]

Teammates who are always looking at the negative are dangerous. They provide the toxic potion of negativity; quietly, freely, and gladly giving cups—and at times buckets—of its destructive poison to their teammates.

Negative team members are also ENERGY SUCKERS, draining every bit of momentum you have. After having a conversation with one of these teammates, you can feel like you just finished 12 rounds with boxing legend Muhammed Ali. Can you relate? I think you would probably agree that most teams need a lot more positive energy and a great deal less of the negative.

Years ago, I was taking a taxicab to the airport with a colleague of mine. We had just concluded what I thought had been a fairly successful meeting. My colleague, however, had a different opinion. The entire ride to the airport was a barrage of negativity directed towards our then new leader. I did not feel the same way as my colleague, and I formed a strong mistrust towards her in some areas for the rest of the time we worked on this team together.

It's one thing to disagree with someone; it is another thing to actively pick out the negative and generalize or label a person's character based on a few things you don't agree with, just as my colleague had done.

When teammates are consistently negative about others, you learn something important about them: *If they are so readily willing to share their negative thoughts about other teammates—especially about people they don't know very well, like my fellow teammate had done on the way to the airport—what would they say about me?*

Teammates quickly lose respect for those who talk negatively about others, as I did for my teammate. A quote I love, which has been attributed to several different people, says: "Great minds discuss ideas. Average minds discuss events. Small minds discuss people"[4]

A close relative to negativity and talking behind someone else's back is gossip. Most people agree that gossiping is wrong and that it is harmful to everyone involved: those spreading the gossip, those hearing the gossip, and, most importantly, those being gossiped about.

A number of years ago, I was brushing my teeth one morning when two of my kids informed me that my two-year old son had used the very toothbrush that I was using the night before! While that may not gross out some people, I am sort of a germ freak and don't like other people's things in my mouth, even if they belong to my kids. That being said, I immediately spit the tainted toothbrush out of my mouth and threw it in the garbage.

Now, my kids could have said they were joking. They could have said my two-year old had never used it, but it didn't matter. That toothbrush would never be the same again. Gossip on teams has the same effect and eventually erodes team trust. Whether it's true or not, it taints a teammate's character and reputation forever, as those on the team hearing the gossip never feel quite the same about whoever is being talked about. In addition, the teammate who is spreading the gossip begins to be trusted less and less by his teammates. It is a lose-lose activity.

Can you do something to stop the negative chain of gossip? Yes!

First, personally commit that you won't participate in gossip. **Second**, when a teammate begins to gossip, many have found the use of the "Triple Filter Test," a technique that has been credited to Socrates, the great philosopher, to be helpful:

One day, a student approached the wise philosopher. "Socrates, I have some news regarding one of your friends," he exclaimed excitedly.

In reply, Socrates said, "Before you tell me this news, let us see if it passes the triple filter test."

"Triple filter test?"

"Yes," said Socrates. "The first test involves **truthfulness**. Tell me, are you certain that what you are going to share with me is absolutely true?"

The man thought for a time and said, "I cannot be sure if it is true, as I heard this news..."

"The second test," Socrates continued, "is of **goodness**. Is your news something good, whether it is true or not?"

"It is actually the opposite..."

Socrates interrupted, "So what you plan to tell me is not true nor good?"

Being slightly embarrassed, the man shrugged his shoulders.

"There is one final test," Socrates continued, "which is that of **usefulness**. Will your news be something that is useful?"
"Not likely," replied the man.

"Well then, if you are going to share something that is neither true nor good nor useful, then there is no reason to tell me at all."[5]

We can —and should—take the time to apply the Triple Filter Test in all of our conversations. This powerful technique would quickly put a stop to gossip on any team.

Another method to stopping the spread of negative gossip is to promote the spread of positive gossip. The Canadian Mental Health Association has suggested that positive gossip can indeed minimize the poisonous spread of negative gossip.[6] You can start by promoting positive gossip yourself. Talk freely about the strengths of others on your team, and celebrate the successes that your teammates have. In other words, be a positive gossip machine! Such positive energy becomes contagious, and soon others on your team will also be spreading positive gossip. Teammates will start looking for the good in each other instead of the negative.

An example of something you might spread includes, "Did you hear how well Mary did on her results today? It's true; she did really well. We sure are lucky to have her on our team. Mary really goes the extra mile in everything she does."

You may also spread something like, "Did you hear that Mark killed it on his sales presentation with the Logo Company on Friday? They liked it so much that they are buying twice what we projected! Can you believe that? He worked so hard. I am really proud of him and glad he is on our team."

Positive gossip beats negative gossip any day, and it almost always passes the triple filter test! Have fun with it, and promote the positive! Positive teammates contagiously create positive teams.

Application: What positive gossip can you begin spreading on your team? What kind of difference would it begin to make on your team if teammates refrained from negativity and instead focused on being positive?

Compliment and Encourage Others

If you are always looking for the good in others, you will also start seeing the good in yourself.

There is an old fable told of a group of frogs that were merrily hopping through the forest. They didn't have a care in the world until two of the frogs fell into a deep pit. All of the other frogs quickly gathered around the large pit and peered down into its great depth. They all began to scratch their heads, trying to come up with a way to help the two frightened frogs.

After some time, the frogs outside of the pit could not think of a solution. They all agreed that it was hopeless for the trapped frogs to try and escape, yelling down to the two frogs that they surely would never get out and should prepare for their fate.

Unwilling to believe the other frogs, the two trapped frogs began jumping, trying to escape the pit. The group of frogs above begin shouting even louder to quit, to give up and that there was no way to get out of there alive. After a period of time, one of the frogs began listening to what his friends were shouting and gave up. The other frog continued jumping.

The shouts of discouragement continued and got louder. Though he was absolutely drained of every bit of energy he had, the determined frog continued to miraculously jump even higher. Eventually, he jumped so high that he sprang right out of the pit. The other frogs celebrated their friend's victory and gathered around him in puzzlement. They said, "Didn't you hear us telling you to stay down, that you wouldn't get out?"

In response, the escaped frog explained that he is hard of hearing and thought the others were telling him to jump higher. "I didn't think you were discouraging me," he said, "I thought you were encouraging me."[7]

Members of teams can change lives by expressing words of encouragement.

A number of years ago, some encouragement and a compliment in a quick conversation with my father changed my life. I had just finished my final research project for my Master's Degree. As part of this process, I had to present and defend my position, which included taking questions from professors and fellow students. The entire thing was fairly stressful, and it was videotaped. Fortunately, I was successful and passed.

I was proud of what I had accomplished and shared the video with my father. When the video was finished, he said, "You ought to consider going into public speaking; you are really good at it."

While I am sure he didn't really think much about what he said, that compliment inspired me to do what I do today, and I have never forgotten it. Since that time, I have delivered hundreds of presentations and workshops, and I have discovered a talent I otherwise would have been unaware of. It only took my father a few seconds to compliment and encourage me, but what he said has stuck with me, even twenty years later. Mark Twain once said, "I can live for two months on a good compliment."[8] I have lived for years on my father's brief and simple compliment.

What kind of impact are your compliments having on your teammates? Have you inspired and encouraged anyone recently?

Complimenting someone is more than just saying something nice; *how* you compliment someone and *how often* you compliment them makes a big difference. I once had a teammate who would regularly say, "You're a good guy." It never felt genuine, and it was lacking in specifics. On top of that, I heard him say the same thing many times to several others on the team! Now, I didn't have an ego that needed to be regularly stroked, but specifically knowing why he felt that way would have made a big difference to me.

Here are four things that are important to consider as part of your quest for delivering compliments:

1. Be Genuine. Give a compliment that you really mean, and never give it with the expectation of getting anything in return. When you are genuine in your compliments, your teammates will see part of your sincerity in the warmth of your eyes and smile. The power of what you say will be felt.

And if you don't mean what you're going to say, don't say it. Receiving a disingenuous compliment feels kind of disheartening, don't you think?

2. Give Specifics. All compliments need to include details and should steer away from feeling "cookie cutter." In addition, the most meaningful comments also include the "how." How did what your teammate do impact you? The "how" should be behind the "why" you are giving the compliment. Doing so creates a more genuine compliment as well.

Saying something like, "Fantastic Job Kristen," doesn't have the same effect as saying, "Scott, I wanted you to know that you did a great job on the XYZ project. I noticed that your attention to detail personally helped me on the project. I heard other teammates comment on it as well."

3. Be Succinct. When saying something nice to a teammate, it is really easy to start rambling if things start to feel awkward. Each person you compliment will receive the compliment a little differently. Some will just smile and simply say, "thank you". Some will try to be humble and deflect the compliment. And some just won't know what to say.

Simply give the compliment in a genuine, specific manner, and move on.

4. Work on Consistency and Balance. There is a balance that needs to be maintained when giving compliments: **giving too few compliments** may feel unnatural for you when you do give them, and **giving too many** will eventually cause others to feel they are insincere.

Now that we have discussed how to give a good compliment, it is important to understand what giving compliments can do for you personally:

- **You start seeing the good in you.** Complimenting others is not only powerfully beneficial to your teammates, but it will change your life as well. Giving genuine compliments requires you to always be searching for the good in others. If you are always looking for the good in others, you will also start seeing the good in yourself.

- **Others see the good in you.** As you help your teammates see the good in themselves, they will reciprocate those good feelings back to you. In essence, you become a magnet of others' genuine compliments. The more you compliment others, the more others will compliment you. It becomes a cycle of giving, receiving, and demonstrating sincere admiration for each other.

- **Your likability and power of influence will increase.** As you genuinely compliment others, your likability and influence rises. Teammates will start wanting to be around you more often, and you will start being seen as a leader on the team. Your ideas, suggestions, and counsel will be listened to more carefully.

- **You feel good.** As you compliment others, you can't help but to feel really good. As was mentioned in Chapter One in reference to service, people are happier when they are doing nice things for others.

Giving compliments is a good habit to practice. I once heard of a CEO that would place five marbles in his right pocket at the beginning of each day. Each time he complimented someone, he would transfer a marble to his left pocket. The goal was that, at the end of the day, he would have transferred all the marbles to his left pocket. Eventually, he didn't need the marbles; complimenting others became a lifelong habit.[9]

Can you imagine if every member of your team followed the prescriptions above? It starts with you. Make up your mind that you will give the gift of genuine, specific, and timely compliments to your teammates, and you will see the difference it can make.

Application: Do you regularly compliment members of your team? If not, why not? Who can you compliment on your team today? Why would it make a positive difference?

Celebrate Success

Being a positive teammate means you celebrate everyone's successes, not just your own.

I once led a team of difficult and strong-willed managers. A practice I strongly encouraged was to celebrate team successes. One particular manager on the team was great at celebrating her own team's achievements (and there were many), but she had a hard time being positive and excited about others' achievements.

In her opinion, there was no greater team than the one she led. Meeting after meeting, her fellow managers heard about all of the great things her team was doing. These other managers were fairly positive about it at first; that is, until it became clear that she only cared about celebrating her own team's success. As a result, the other managers on this team began to resent her, talk bad about her and avoided working with her. This was not a good recipe for our team's success.

How do you feel about the success of others on your team? Are you happy or envious? Excited or jealous? Do you celebrate them, or ignore them? Part of being a positive teammate means that you celebrate the successes of all your teammates.

How did you feel the last time someone celebrated something you did well? Leadership author and friend of mine Mark Macy tells the following story of an experience he had with a basketball team he was asked to coach and a player affectionately referred to as "Bookworm":

My phone rang; it was a call from the Parks and Recreation Department asking me to coach a fifth-grade girls' basketball team. After a short discussion, I found out it was a "left over" group of six girls from several schools that didn't get put on a team because the league had already filled all of their team rosters.

Anyone who has coached knows that it takes at least five decent players, plus a couple of "stars," to win some games. The Parks and Rec leader informed me that with this team, the season would be a long one. He also said to not feel bad if we did not win a single game. "Just make sure they all get to play in each game," he said.

As part of our discussion, I convinced the Parks and Rec department to allow me to recruit at least one additional player so I could start the season with seven players. Two of the seven had actually played before, four knew what a basketball was, and the other one had parents who had made her join as a way for her get out to expand her experiences. For lack of a better name, I will refer to this last player as "Bookworm".

We began practice at a local gym a couple of times a week, starting with the basics and working up to a very simple defense and offense.

We even learned an in-bounds play (getting the ball from outside the line of play and into the court).

As we practiced, I could tell that Bookworm was having a very difficult time. Her basketball skills were primitive at best. She couldn't shoot the ball high enough from any point on the floor to hit the net, let alone go through the basket. Her mother actually came up to me in private and asked what she could do to help her outside of practice. I gave her some very simple drills to try, thinking that at the very least they could keep her from getting hurt on the court when she did get to play.

Soon enough, the first game came. By some miracle, we actually won by a couple of points. We went on to win four in a row! In each of those games, I had been crafty in how much I let Bookworm play. I tried to hide her from a lot of interaction, trying to keep any potential embarrassment to a minimum.

I knew that there would be a game where Bookworm would actually get her hands on a ball, and if she touched the ball, a foul would likely be called. At that point, Bookworm would go to the line and eventually be embarrassed because she couldn't even lift the ball higher than four feet. I could not let that happen.

As a solution, I focused on just having her shoot free throws practice after practice. I finally figured out that having her shoot "granny style" (shooting under the hands as opposed to on top of the hands) might be the only way to lift the ball high enough to at least get it close to the rim.

The game finally came where Bookworm got a rebound, and, you guessed it, she was fouled. The referee signaled two shots and showed her where the shooting line was. Her little legs and hands were shaking, her head was down, and she was scared to death. I called time-out.

As she stood there in the huddle, I clutched her hands to keep them from trembling and expressed my belief that she was going to do just great. I reminded her about the many hours of practice she had, and we reviewed what she had learned about shooting "granny style." Her teammates expressed confidence in her. The huddle broke, and she went back to the free throw line. It appeared that she was not as nervous, but she definitely did not have the swagger of a person who knows they will make the shot.

As she set up and launched her shot, I prayed, "God, let it please hit the rim!" The ball rose up and up and, to my surprise, even past the height of the net. Then the miracle occurred: the ball went right in - nothing but net. Swish!

She was shocked! The crowd went crazy! I stood there in disbelief. I called time-out again! Why? So we could celebrate as a team and enjoy the moment together. All season, we had worked hard and were fortunate to have celebrated in many team successes. Now, it was time to bask and celebrate in Bookworm's success. A miracle like this might not ever happen again.

The story doesn't end there. She then went back to the line for her second shot. This time, she wasn't dragging her feet or had her head down; instead, she walked with a swagger of confidence I've never seen from her. She took the ball, went through the same routine, and she ripped the ball through the hoop a second time!

I called a time-out again! Why? So, we could celebrate again! Those were the only two points Bookworm made that year.[10]

This story makes you feel good, doesn't it? You can imagine the joy of every person on that team, stars and non-stars alike, who were genuinely excited for Bookworm's success.

Celebrating a teammate' success doesn't have to be elaborate. Though it could have the feeling of a party with balloons, streamers etc., it can also be as simple as genuinely telling someone how happy, proud, and/or excited you are for them. In Bookworm's case, it was as simple as calling a timeout.

When we celebrate another's success, something happens to us. It's much like the "Service Effect" discussed in Chapter One: The more we serve, the more we love; the more we love, the more desire we have to serve. The more we celebrate others, the more we appreciate and love others; the more we appreciate and love others, the more desire we will have to celebrate all of their successes.

Samuel Goldwyn, a Jewish Polish American film producer, put it this way: "When someone does something well, applaud! You will make two people happy."[11]

Application: What successes are your teammates having that you can celebrate? Why would celebrating the successes of your teammates be a good thing?

YOU ARE THE TEAM

5. Be Respectful

As you strive to respect teammates, your teammates will do the same for you.

An unknown author once shared a story about a short-tempered little boy who lived in a village long ago. His father decided to teach him a lesson by giving him a bag of nails and telling him that he was required to hammer one nail into the backyard fence every time he lost his temper.

Over the next several weeks, the little boy had hammered in 37 nails! However, as the weeks progressed, he was driving in fewer and fewer nails as he learned to control his outbursts. Eventually, the boy learned how to control his temper most of the time. His father was proud and suggested that the boy pull out one nail for every day that he completely controlled his temper.

Many days passed, and the boy went to tell his father that all of the nails were now removed from the fence. The wise father took his son by the hand, and they walked over to the fence. He said, "Great job, son; you have done really well, and I am very proud of you! But I want you to notice the holes. This fence will never be the same. When you say things in anger, you leave a scar, just like you have left scars in this fence."

From that day forward, the boy was even more determined never to lose his temper again.[1]

When teammates are unkind, fail to understand one another, or lack empathy, they run the risk of hammering their own nails and leaving holes that can't be easily repaired. Successful teamwork is based on the team's ability to cooperate. Cooperation is based on the respect that team members have for each other. If you understand the nature of teamwork and if you have the desire to make the team better, you understand the need and obligation to respect the members of your team.

Is this always easy? Of course not, but your own personal effort to respect your teammates makes a difference. You don't necessarily always have to like all members of your team, but you can show respect, be kind, and try to understand them. Respect can start with you. As you strive to respect teammates, your teammates will do the same for you. As a result, cooperation and understanding will increase, and teamwork will improve.

Extend Kindness

Extending kindness might be a small thing for you, but can be big thing for a teammate.

May 2010 was one of the most difficult months of my life. My mother had passed away somewhat unexpectedly around Mother's Day. She was the matriarch and center of our family. After her passing, many people wrote kind notes about my mother, many of which I saved.

I always knew my mom was very, very special, but I had no idea how she had affected so many lives. People kindly shared with me countless stories about how she had changed their lives due to her generosity, kindness, and example.

Since that time, I have unfortunately been to my share of funerals, including my father's, and I have observed that many who pass on were really wonderful people. Why do we wait until people are gone to recognize how truly wonderful they are? Why don't we shower others with our kind thoughts more often?

Everyone has good in them and everyone deserves kindness, just as the following inspirational story of one kind champion demonstrates:

Meghan Vogel had just won the 1,600-meter title in the Ohio Division III girls state meet. However, what she did in her next race earned her a 2012 National Sportsmanship Award.

Less than an hour after her 1600-meter race, Vogel participated in the 3200-meter race. She was running out of energy and fell into last place. As she rounded the final turn, Vogal watched as Arden McMath (someone Vogel had never met before) collapsed in front of her. Vogel had never finished last in a race, and this opponent's fall provided the perfect opportunity to keep that record. However, instead of running past Mcmath, Meghan Vogel came to her aid.

She said, "I remember moving to her position. [McMath] was doing the best she could to keep her body upright. There was a lot of shake in her legs, which is totally understandable."[2]

Vogal carried McMath down the final stretch, making sure to keep her opponent in front of her. The crowd's cheering grew louder as the two approached the finish, and Vogel guided McMath across the finish line ahead of her. The crowd, touched by the kindness they had just been so privileged to watch, gave them both a standing ovation.

Vogel told WDTN news at the time, "If you work to get to the state meet, you deserve to finish no matter who you are. I was going to make it happen for her no matter what."[3]

YOU ARE THE TEAM

One generous act of kindness created an act of teamwork as the two girls worked together to finish their race. Being there for others—including teammates and opponents—improves relationships, which improves all of us.

To help you show greater kindness in a specific and personal way to your teammates, try following these five tips. Doing so will make a big difference for you, in your team, and in your organization.

1. Smile. There is something powerful about a warm smile.

A number of years ago, our family went on a vacation to a small amusement park about four hours from where we lived. We had younger children, so we spent a lot of time on rides for kids.

It was close to 100 degrees outside, a little humid, and there were kids screaming, crying, yelling, and laughing everywhere… you get the picture. Being a ride operator in this part of the park can require a lot of patience and hard work, as was evident on the faces of just about every young ride operator there; all, that is, except for one.

The exception was a young girl of about 16 or 17. As the kids rode her ride, she had a pleasant and kind smile. It was contagious; I found myself smiling as well. You could tell she enjoyed the kids, her job, and was genuinely happy. Her noticeable happiness made me happier. I doubt this young ride operator had any idea the influence she was having, but she was making a difference.

Have you ever had a teammate who made you happier because of a smile? Something even as simple as a smile can make a world of difference on your team. It can make you happy, others happy, and it takes fewer muscles than frowning! Mother Teresa once said, "We shall never know all the good that a simple smile can do."[4]

2. Say "Please," "Thank You," and "You Are Welcome." These are simple words, but people will notice when you say them, and they can make a big difference.

Gayle LaSalle, CEO of Accountability at LaSalle Consulting and Training, shared the following story on my blog several years ago, and it has stuck with me ever since:

"A few years ago, I was having lunch with my 3-year-old granddaughter and her mom. She has been taught to say thank you when someone does something for you. She said, "thank you' to the waiter who simply walked away. She looked at her mom and said, 'He didn't say you're welcome.' If a 3-year-old notices, you can be sure others do as well."[5]

When we fail to be kind with politeness, others do take notice.

3. Truly Listen. My wife has a lot of friends that consider her a very good friend, if not a best friend. It has always amazed me how easily she attracts people to her. It is all in her ability to truly listen to others and take a genuine interest in their lives. She is more interested in others than trying to be interesting.

Many of us, on the other hand, love to talk about ourselves, offer our opinions on topics of personal interest, and solve others' problems without truly listening to what is being said. We love being interesting to others instead of taking an interest in them. And if something isn't interesting to us and we don't have anything interesting to say about ourselves, we stop listening.

Years ago, I was in the office of a teammate and friend. I was sharing something personal about a recent challenge I was having and being somewhat vulnerable. As I was talking, my teammate reached for his phone and started checking his email! I didn't know I could be so boring, but I also didn't realize he could be so insensitive. I immediately changed the topic and then kindly excused myself. After this experience, I would never share anything personal with this teammate again.

Being kind requires us to respect teammates enough to listen carefully to them.

4. Just Say It. If you are thinking something kind about a teammate, then share it. Just like the experience I had with receiving notes about my mother after her passing that I shared in the chapter introduction, we don't share our kind thoughts enough. There are few things that quickly endear people to others more than sharing kind thoughts.

If you appreciate a comment a teammate made in a meeting, say it. If you really admire a certain trait that a teammate has, say it. If you think a teammate really goes the extra mile, say it. Ralph Waldo Emerson said, "You cannot do a kindness too soon, for you never know how soon it will be too late."[6]

5. Do Kind Acts. As we discussed more extensively in Chapter One, the power of service is huge. Doing nice things for others without expecting anything in return can lift both the giver and the receiver. Don't ask what you can get from others; instead, ask what you can give.

Kindness changes people. Leo Buscaglia, an American Author and educator once wrote, "Too often we underestimate the power of a touch, a smile, a kind word, a listening ear, an honest compliment, or the smallest act of caring, all of which have the potential to turn a life around."[7]

Do you want to inspire and help people become better? If so, then try a little kindness. Extending kindness might be a small thing for you, but can be a big thing for a teammate.

Application: If your teammates were asked how kind you are, what would they say? Why would they respond that way? What can you start doing to extend more kindness?

Seek to Understand

We would all be wise to actively understand others first.

There is an old Welsh fable told of a dog that belonged to Llywelyn the Great, a Prince of Gwynedd in the 13th century. Prince Llywelyn's wife had passed away, and his faithful dog was charged with watching the cradle of the Prince's baby while the Prince was gone hunting.

After one particular hunting trip, Prince Llywelyn returned home to find his baby's cradle overturned. With his baby missing and his dog's mouth covered with blood, the Prince plunged his sword into the dog with the idea that it had killed his baby.

The dog's dying yelp was answered by a child's cry. Prince Llywelyn searched and found the baby, unharmed and laying near the dead body of a mighty wolf. The Prince's dog had actually protected the baby as his owner had desired.

It is said that the Prince was filled with such remorse that he never smiled again.[8]

This story makes a good point, though a fairly dramatic one: making quick judgments and jumping to conclusions can lead to regrets—sometimes very large regrets. Unfortunately, it is all too common to tell ourselves stories without all of the facts. Instead of seeking to understand, we often seek first to condemn.

On a team, the ugly consequences of such quick judgments can result in the creation of team clicks and less team unity—which, like the dog in the story, can quickly lead to a team's demise. To help avoid making your own quick judgments about teammates, try practicing the following three tips. You will find that the application of these tips increases team trust, respect, and unity.

1. Take a Break. When we are frustrated, it is wise and respectful to wait before tackling a difficult situation. If Prince Llywelyn had waited just a minute or two before slaying his dog, the outcome would have been very different.

When we hear and create stories about others based on limited information, it can be easy to not only believe them but also defend them at all costs. It can become increasingly difficult to separate facts from our own emotions, including those of worry, disappointment, hurt feelings, and anger. If you find this happening to you, simply take a deep breath and separate yourself from any negative emotions you are experiencing.

Several years ago, I sat in a parent meeting for my son who was playing high school basketball. After the head coach had talked about policies, schedules, etc., the school Athletic Director spoke. He pleaded with parents to follow what he called the "24 Hour Rule."

"Whenever you have a gripe with a coach, don't approach him right after the game," he said. "If you do, the coach may act in a way he shouldn't, which may cause you to act in a way you shouldn't."

Instead, he suggested that parents wait 24 hours before bringing up an issue with the coach. This gives parents a chance to sleep on the problem and then deal with it in a more levelheaded way. Likewise, there will be times when it is best to take a walk around the building before discussing something with a teammate. This has personally worked for me many times. It is amazing how your perspective can change when you separate yourself from the situation for a bit.

2. Assume Positively. Another way to avoid jumping to conclusions is to assume positive intent. Respect your teammates enough to give them the benefit of the doubt. But this is easier said than done, as I learned years ago.

One morning, I was taking my kids to school. As I was driving down the long road from the hill on which we lived, someone was tailgating behind me. I am not fond of people who tailgate, so I began to create a lot of stories in my head about why the "jerk" behind me was following so closely. In short, I was completely jumping to conclusions.

Eventually, I was so frustrated that I pulled over. When I did, I noticed that the person who was on my bumper and now speeding past me was actually my neighbor! My whole attitude changed. Instead of being angry, I wondered if everything was okay because my neighbor would never do anything to deliberately make me angry.

Because I knew my neighbor and his character, it was easier for me to let go of the frustration that came with him tailgating me. Likewise, it is a lot easier to give your teammates the benefit of the doubt when you know and understand them. Building relationships with team members is an important key to trusting them and not jumping to conclusions. It also makes it easier to assume positive intent.

3. Identify Truth. I love a cartoon I once saw of a large, smiling, red fish getting ready to take a big bite of bait on a fisherman's line. The caption read, "Sometimes it is better to keep your mouth shut!" As team members, we would all be wise to do the same by patiently seeking the truth before opening our mouths!

To help identify the truth, you could ask questions like, *How did I create this story and come to this conclusion? Did it originate from something that I was told by someone who was not directly involved with the situation?* Oftentimes, it does. Perhaps it is a story you created by observing something that seemed a little out of place. No matter how the story came about, you can avoid jumping to conclusions by talking directly to the source; anything else is most likely some form of gossip from someone who has little credibility, or from your own interpretation, which, in my experience, is often wrong.

One of the barriers to communication today is the lack of it. In fact, it is probably the number-one source of all misunderstanding. Speak directly with your teammates to understand them, and your results will be one of two outcomes: either what you heard is true, or it isn't. Either way, you now have the truth!

No matter what we may hear around the office or within our teams, we would all be wise to actively seek to understand others first.

Application: What changes do you need to make in your life to try to understand others better and avoid jumping to conclusions. Why would that be important?

Demonstrate Empathy

Each of us experience sadness and deal with difficult challenges, regardless of how "tough" we might appear.

A number of years ago, my young family and I had spent the day before Christmas Eve at Disneyland because we were told it wouldn't be crowded. Whoever told us that was wrong! It was hot, very crowded, and I was grumpy. I was also being very critical of others. It seemed like most of the teenagers at the park were "troublemakers," decked out in their backward caps, low-hanging pants, and white cotton tank tops. I made judgments on their character based on things I had recently seen in the news and in my neighborhood. I have to sadly admit that I wasn't a very pleasant person to be around that day.

The next day, on Christmas Eve, we were driving to my parents' house when we came upon an accident. A car had caught fire, and there were people inside the vehicle, unaware of the smoke billowing from the back of it. I told my wife to take the car and the kids to a safe place. I then ran to the vehicle to help the passengers get out and over to a safe place across the street.

What I saw next taught me something I will never forget:

There, sitting on the curb with backward caps, low-hanging pants, and white cotton tank tops, now with tears streaming down their eyes, was a group of the very same type of teenagers I had made snide remarks about the day before; however, this time, my attitude changed. I had no snide remarks, only compassion and relief that they were safe.

I learned something remarkable that day: none of us are immune from adversity in our lives. **Each of us experience sadness and deal with difficult challenges, regardless of how "tough" we might appear.** We all have pain; some just hide it better than others. As Plato once said, "Be kind, for everyone you meet is fighting a hard battle."[9] That Christmas Eve, I became a different person. I became a better husband, a better father, a better teammate and a better leader.

Empathy is foundational to our team relationships. Empathy is trying to see the world from another's eyes or to take a walk in someone else's shoes. It helps us understand why someone does what they do. It also allows us to have greater patience, understanding, and compassion when we are working with others.

A video by the Cleveland Clinic titled, "Empathy: The Human Connection to Patient Care," beautifully portrays the different emotions, challenges, and trials that the Clinic's patients and staff encounter each day. The video starts with a worried man being wheeled into the hospital with the caption, "Has been dreading this appointment. Fears he waited too long."

Next, the video pans to a younger man walking out of the hospital, the caption saying, "Wife's surgery went well. Going home to rest."

The video then quickly moves to show a reflective, older woman sitting in a hospital gown, hooked up to an oxygen tank. The caption reads, "Day 29. Waiting for a new heart."

In the next scene, a father approaches his deeply concerned and distraught wife with a cup of coffee, the caption reading, "19-year-old son on life support."

The video continues by showing patients who do not completely understand what the doctor is saying, and those who are too shocked to comprehend treatment options. It depicts a frustrated man who has been in the waiting room for three hours. At another point, the video depicts three people in an elevator: a concerned older man whose wife had a stroke and he wonders how he will take care of her, a hospital staff member who is recently divorced, and a smiling doctor who just found out he is going to be a new father.

On and on, the video continues showing patients, visitors, and staff with captions of both the difficult and the good things that are happening in their lives. The purpose of this video is to help the staff of the Cleveland Clinic to see what those around them are experiencing on a day-to-day basis. By being more aware of what others are experiencing, staff members might just be a little kinder, a little more compassionate, and exercise a little more patience, all of which are positive outcomes of empathy.

As a description of their video, the Cleveland Clinic states that "patient care is more than just healing—it's building a connection that encompasses mind, body and soul. If you could stand in someone else's shoes . . . hear what they hear. See what they see. Feel what they feel. Would you treat them differently?"[10]

In most teams, you interact with your teammates as they pass you in the break room, engage with you in meetings, and directly work with you on projects; yet, even with all of this contact, you may be unaware of their history or challenges. *If a video was made of your team, what would it look like? What would the captions say? Are you really trying to understand others?*

As a parent, I have raised five teenagers, and I am in the process of raising three more—*sigh* (actually, I love it!). I have been frustrated many times by my teenagers' reasoning, lack of judgment, or inability to solve their own problems (I know some of you can relate). As I look back, there have been many times I just didn't understand them. But when I took a deep breath and remembered myself as a teenager, I suddenly had a better understanding and greater patience. It only took a minute to realize that I used to be just like them - that's what empathy does.

It might only take you a minute, as well, to demonstrate greater empathy towards your teammates. We relate best to people who are like us; if they are not like us, we sometimes quickly—and sometimes harshly—make unfair judgments. Next time, however, do as the old Amish proverb states: "Instead of putting others in their place, put yourself in their place."[11]

Application: What types of challenges are your teammates having? How can you put yourself in their shoes to better understand them? What kind of difference would it make on your team if teammates started showing more empathy?

YOU ARE THE TEAM

6. Be Great

It is by the steady application of small and simple things that we become great.

M. Russell Ballard, an American religious leader, once told the following story:

"Oftentimes we are like the young merchant from Boston, who in 1849, as the story goes, was caught up in the fervor of the California gold rush. He sold all of his possessions to seek his fortune in the California rivers, which he was told were filled with gold nuggets so big that one could hardly carry them.

"Day after endless day, the young man dipped his pan into the river and came up empty. His only reward was a growing pile of rocks. Discouraged and broke, he was ready to quit until one day an old, experienced prospector said to him, 'That's quite a pile of rocks you are getting there, my boy.'

"The young man replied, 'There's no gold here. I'm going back home.'

"Walking over to the pile of rocks, the old prospector said, 'Oh, there is gold all right. You just have to know where to find it.' He picked two rocks up in his hands and crashed them together. One of the rocks split open, revealing several flecks of gold sparkling in the sunlight.

"Noticing a bulging leather pouch fastened to the prospector's waist, the young man said, 'I'm looking for nuggets like the ones in your pouch, not just tiny flecks.'

"The old prospector extended his pouch toward the young man, who looked inside, expecting to see several large nuggets. He was stunned to see that the pouch was filled with thousands of flecks of gold.

"The old prospector said, 'Son, it seems to me you are so busy looking for large nuggets that you're missing filling your pouch with these precious flecks of gold. The patient accumulation of these little flecks has brought me great wealth."[1]

Like the young merchant, it's not uncommon to think that greatness is achieved by finally getting that big promotion, an important project, or that one large account. The reality is that greatness is achieved by the accumulation of many smaller things. "Overnight successes" are, in fact, not overnight for most, but small successes over many nights.

Like learning to play the piano (or anything for that matter), it is the patient discipline of practice and the accumulation of many simple successes that takes a pianist from playing *Twinkle, Twinkle Little Star* to Chopin's *Waltz in C sharp minor, Op. 64, No. 2.*

Everything you have read up to this point has led to this concluding chapter: Be Great. If you commit to being more selfless, trustworthy, humble, positive, and respectful, you are well on your way to becoming a great teammate. These attributes are small and simple things in and of themselves, but over time they collectively become big things as you practice and apply them on a regular basis. It is by the steady application of small and simple things that we become great.

In this chapter, we are going to talk about a few additional principles that make teammates great, such as working hard and going the extra mile; understanding your team's goals, vision, and your unique contribution; actively searching for solutions to team problems; and being passionately involved in your own personal development.

The good news is that most of you already have some gold in your pouches—you are on your way to becoming great. All you need is just a little more commitment and a little more focus and/or discipline. Now is the time to take what you already have and make something even greater out of it.

It is my personal belief that most of us live far below what we are capable of becoming. I love the following quote by Wilma Rudolph, a past Olympic and international star, "Never underestimate the power of dreams and the influence of the human spirit. We are all the same in this notion: The potential for greatness lives within each of us."[2]

The potential for greatness lives in you! By being great, you are like the old prospector in the story above. Over time, you are patiently creating great wealth for yourself; but in addition to your personal wealth, you are also bringing great value and wealth to your team! Make the commitment today to be great!

Get It Done, and Then Some

In order to expect the best from your team, you have to expect the best from yourself.

There is an old football story told of a critical game between two very different teams. The larger team was winning, though the score stayed fairly close throughout the contest. As the game was nearing the end, the coach of the smaller and outmatched team knew his only hope to win was to give the ball to the best running back on the field: Calhoun. This speedy running back could outmaneuver and outrun anyone trying to tackle him.

The coach called a timeout and drew up four plays for the team, instructing the quarterback to give the ball to Calhoun every time and let him work his magic against their very large and physical opponent. On the first play, everyone watched with great anticipation, but Calhoun didn't get the ball. On the second play, everyone was hoping Calhoun would get the ball, but, once again, he didn't.

There were only seconds left in the game, and the team's only hope was that Calhoun would get the ball and run the length of the field for the touchdown. However, just like in the last two plays, Calhoun never got the ball. By this time, the coach was extremely angry and reminded his quarterback, once again, to give the ball to Calhoun.

When it was time for the fourth play, however, the quarterback was tackled and the game ended. Furious, the coach got up in the quarterback's face and yelled, "I told you to give the ball to Calhoun four times, and now we've lost the game!"

The quarterback looked his coach in the eyes and, standing tall, told him, "I called the play four times to give the ball to Calhoun, just as you asked coach. The problems is that Calhoun 'don't want the ball.'"[3]

Sometimes, team members just don't want the ball. It's not because they can't perform and get the job done; instead, for some reason, they simply choose to not take the ball. Unfortunately, many team members live far below what they are capable of accomplishing. When they have an opportunity to take the ball, they don't. Or when they are given the ball, they quickly give it to someone else—or drop it all together. They may also just simply wait for more directions on what to do with the ball or only do the bare minimum.

Every team benefits from teammates who want the ball. These kinds of teammates raise their hand when an opportunity is presented. They don't wait for someone else to step up and get the job done. They are the type of teammates who receive a difficult assignment and don't immediately look for ways to pawn it off to someone else or drop it all together. These teammates don't have to wait for more direction before taking action. Are you a teammate who wants the ball, who goes above and beyond what is required of you?

What I am really asking is, are you perceived as a star performer on your team, or are you considered a burden to the team? Are you a "get it done and then some" kind of contributor, or are you an "I'm not done and hopefully, maybe, cross my fingers, it will get done" kind of contributor? If the former, keep up the good work and keep improving! If the latter, you can change that. The first step to changing and improving is honestly answering the above questions. By doing so, you will have a better sense of what type of team contributor you are.

In order to expect the best from your team, you have to expect the best from yourself. The team can't become great without team members trying to become great on their own. Greatness starts with you. You can't control what others do, but you can always control your own effort. Wake up each day with the goal of being better than the day before. Even just one percent better will move you to becoming that much greater. As you work towards becoming greater, the entire team becomes better because of it.

Becoming an excellent team member is mainly achieved through small and simple things. You have to be willing to take a step beyond the standard in all that you do, one degree here and another degree there. It's giving just a little more effort every day.

I love the following riddle I once heard: There are 5 frogs sitting on a lily pad. 1 frog decides to jump off. How many frogs are left? Most would say the answer is 4. But look more closely; the real answer is 5. Why? Because the one only **decided** to jump off; he didn't actually **do** it.[4]

Becoming better and getting things done and then some requires more than just deciding to do so. You must do it. In today's world, there are many dreamers, there are some believers, and there are very few doers. Make up your mind to be a doer, and then prove it.

Teams and organizations love and benefit greatly from having doers on their team. Doers are teammates that you can depend on, that are always ready to pitch in and are always involved. They are leaders, and they don't wait in the background to be told what to do. Instead, they already have their sleeves rolled up and are ready to get to work before a word is even said. They have an uncanny ability to recognize when something needs to be done and then getting it done.

Now, don't let this description scare you off. Contrary to what you may think, doers are not necessarily more gifted and talented than everyone else. Instead, they simply just care more. The reality is that anyone can be a doer if they put their mind to it.

One of the most powerful catalysts to great teamwork is a doer. Doers can raise the bar for everyone else. A perfect example of this comes from the inspirational story of how one man achieved what was once thought to be an unattainable milestone:

For years, experts said it was impossible to run a mile in less than four minutes—the human body just wasn't capable of doing it, they said. Year after year, runners tried to do the impossible and prove the scientists wrong, but they always came up short.

During the 1940's, several runners came close to reaching the four-minute mile. Some came as close as one second away, but no one could quite break four minutes. Many thought that the human body had reached its limit. That is, until May 6, 1954. On this day, a 25-year-old medical student from England, Roger Bannister, ran the mile in 3:59.4. Since that time, the four-minute mile has become a standard for all middle-distance runners and has since been lowered 17 seconds![5]

When one performer rises to the top, others will soon follow. Be the "get it done, and then some" kind of player on your team. As you become great, others will become great as well. What was once thought to be impossible will become possible, which is what greatness is all about!

Application: Are you a "get it done and then some" type of teammate? If not, why not? What can you start doing differently to raise the bar on your team?

Know Where You Are Going

Great teammates understand the vision and goals of the team, and they understand the contribution that they and others make to achieve them.

There is a fable about a Mayor who decided to take a walk across the park on a windy March day. On this walk, he came upon a small boy who was flying the biggest and most spectacular kite he had ever seen. It soared high and gently across the sky, so much so that the Mayor was sure it could be seen in the next city.

The Mayor's little town didn't have very many spectacular things, so he decided to award a "key to the city" to the one responsible for setting such a beautiful scene. "Who is responsible for flying this kite?" the Mayor asked.

"I am," said the young boy as he held on to the beautiful, large kite with all his might. "I made this huge kite myself, with my own hands. I painted all of the colorful pictures on it, and I fly it!"

The wind disagreed. "I am," it said. "It is my breeze that keeps this kite in the air, flying so big and so beautifully. Unless I blow on it, the kite will not fly. I fly it!"

"Not true," claimed the kite's tail. "I make the kite sail, making it stable against the wind's blowing gusts. Without me, the kite would spin and crash to the earth. I fly the kite!"

So, who flies the kite?[6]

They all do, don't they? While the boy, the wind, and the tail understand how they each personally contribute to flying the kite, it is a little unclear to them how the rest of the players contribute to making the kite soar high! Great teammates understand the vision and goals of the team, and they understand the contribution that they and others make to achieve them.

If you do not understand your team's vision and goals, nor yours and others' unique contributions, it will be difficult to become great. Not knowing your team's vision and goals is like being in a rowboat in the middle of a lake that is covered by dense and heavy fog. You are being told to keep rowing, but you have no idea where you are going. How long do you think you will keep rowing? Or at the very least, will you continue to row with the same vigor and energy you had at the start if you are unsure of the destination?

When you are unclear on the team's vision and goals, it can be difficult to know just how you and others directly contribute. Without knowing how you affect your team goals, it is going to be a long and frustrating journey to nowhere! Great teammates are clear on the team's overall vision and goals, and they demonstrate complete loyalty to them. They are rowing with all of their might and encouraging others to do so as well.

If the vision and team goals aren't clear, or if you aren't doing enough to help your team get there, here are three things you can do to change your situation:

1. Ask. This one is simple. If you aren't sure what your team's vision and goals are, or if they are somewhat unclear, then ask. Go to your leader and get on the same page. Ask how your leader sees or has seen you significantly contributing to your team's vision and goals. What is the most important thing you do that makes the team great?

In addition, ask your teammates what they consider their role to be on the team. Each member of your team plays a unique part in realizing the vision and goals of the team. Knowing one another's uniqueness to the team and each other's expectations ensures stronger collaboration, communication, and movement towards the vision and goals. It's really about everyone getting on the same page and rowing in the same direction.

2. Think. In the spirit of "getting it done and then some," once you understand what your role is, it's not enough to become comfortable and simply row at the same pace you always have. Start thinking about how you can contribute beyond others' expectations. How can your unique gifts and talents take your team to the next level in reaching your goals and vision?

3. Do. It's all in the execution. You can have great ideas, but until you act upon those ideas, they aren't really all that great. This old fable illustrates the importance of doing instead of just thinking:

"Once upon a time, the only thing that stood between complete happiness and a house full of mice was a big and mean old cat. One night the mice got together and decided to do some brainstorming.

"They asked 'How can we deal with the danger of the cat?' They voted on one brilliant idea that was proposed.

"They would hang a bell around the cat's neck. Wherever the cat would go, the bell would warn them of danger if it got too close.

"Each of the mice jumped and clapped in approval at the brilliant idea. That was until one mouse asked, 'Now who is going to hang the bell around the cat's neck?" There was complete silence."[7]

It is easy to come up with brilliant ideas, but it's another thing to actually execute them. Arnold H. Glasow, an American Businessman and author, once said, "An idea not coupled with action will never get any bigger than the brain cell it occupied."[8]

Once you understand your team's vision, your unique contribution, and how you can use your uniqueness to help your team reach its goals and realize its vision, then it is time to do something about it. How hard and smart you row takes on a new purpose when you know where you are going and what your and your team's role is in getting there.

Application: What are your team's vision and goals? How are you and others on your team uniquely contributing to them? What can you do to become clearer?

Bring Solutions

Being a great teammate means you bring solutions to the team, not problems.

Few have ever heard of Nicholas Winton. He was a humble man with a huge accomplishment that wouldn't be recognized by the world until 50 years later.

Mr. Winton was a London stockbroker, and in December of 1938, he was looking forward to a Swiss skiing vacation when a friend asked him to forgo his planned trip and visit him in Czechoslovakia to rescue Jewish children. At that time, Britain had a program called "Kindertransport," which sent representatives to Germany and Austria to rescue Jewish children, saving 10,000 before World War II started.

In Czechoslovakia, however, there was no such mass effort for rescuing Jewish children. So, in response to this lack of effort, Mr. Winton got to work and created his own rescue program. It involved a great deal of time, work, ingenuity, and courage to accomplish.

The *New York Times'* obituary of Nicholas Winton read, "[Winton's rescue efforts] involved dangers, bribes, forgery, secret contacts with the Gestapo, nine railroad trains, an avalanche of paperwork and a lot of money. Nazi agents started following him. In his Prague hotel room, he met terrified parents desperate to get their children to safety, although it meant surrendering them to strangers in a foreign land."[9]

Through his efforts, Nicholas Winton saved a total of 669 children from the Holocaust. To this day, these children call themselves "Winton's Children."

Knighted by Queen Elizabeth II in 2003, Sir Nicholas Winton was a hero. Not many knew of Nicholas Winton, and even fewer knew of the breadth of his accomplishments. His wife wasn't even aware of the extent of his heroism, that is, until 1988 when she found an old scrapbook in the attic containing the names of the children he rescued, their parents' names, and the names and addresses of the host families.

When Winton's wife brought the scrapbook to his attention, Winton suggested she throw it out, thinking it had no value. Of course, she didn't. Instead, she gave the scrapbook to a Holocaust historian, and we now have this wonderful and inspiring story of this humble leader.

No one needed to ask Sir Nicholas Winton to take action. He saw a problem and found a way to use his talents and skills to bless the lives of hundreds. That's what leaders do. That's what you can do, too.

When asked in an interview by the *New York Times* in 2001 why he did what he did, Winton simply and humbly said, "One saw the problem there, that a lot of these children were in danger, and you had to get them to what was called a safe haven, and there was no organization to do that."[10]

Sir Nicholas Winton is a personal hero of mine. I love that he didn't wait for someone to tell him what to do. I love that he didn't wait for someone else to start a rescue program. I love that he saw a problem, found a solution, and went to work, risking his own life to save hundreds of others in the process. He didn't just talk about the problem, nor did he just wish that someone else would take care of the problem. He did something about the problem.

Sir Nicholas Winton knew what it meant to be great, though he most likely wouldn't have admitted it.

Being a great teammate means you bring solutions to the team. Often times, we think that all we need to do when there is a problem is bring it up to our manager. Sure, it is important to be transparent about problems and bring them to the attention of others. However, it is more important to bring solutions—that's why you are on a team.

So, how can you start bringing solutions and not just problems? Try following these four simple steps:

1. Start with the problem. Do you clearly understand what the problem is? Without understanding the problem, you may not realize there really *isn't* a problem at all, or that the problem really isn't what you think it is. You might, for example, believe that there is a problem with your supplier because they aren't getting your team the widgets you ordered quickly enough. It turns out, however, that the problem has more to do with the purchasing department waiting too long to order.

By understanding the problem, you can save yourself the embarrassment of going to your leader and/or team with a problem that doesn't exist.

2. Diagnose what is going wrong. Now that you understand what the problem is, the question is, why is it happening? What is the root cause of the problem? If we go back to our example with the purchasing department, is the delay in ordering a result of being overloaded with other orders? Is it because they don't understand the expectations around the process flow? Or is it because they simply don't care? Start digging into the real reason behind the delay. Correctly diagnosing the problem allows you to bring solutions to your leader and/or team. Simply ask, *why?*

3. Bring solutions. Now that you have diagnosed the problem, suggest solutions of what you think will solve it. In your solution, include the time, cost, and other details that will be required to fix the problem. Be sure to bring **all possible** solutions to the leader and/or team.

4. Be prepared to fix it. As you bring solutions, don't simply leave them with your leader and/or team; instead, talk about what you can do personally to fix what's wrong. Be a doer—your leader and team will appreciate it. This is the "get it done and then some" approach we discussed earlier in the chapter.

Like Sir Nicholas Winton, if you see there is a problem, find a solution and then go to work to make it happen.

Application: Do you simply bring problems to the attention of your leader and/or team and why? Or are you also bringing solutions? How can you change your approach to be more solution focused?

Develop Yourself

It may require discipline; it won't always be convenient, and the effort might not seem worth it at times. But making your own self-development a priority is a critical investment with a guaranteed payoff.

Not too many years ago, I reflected on something that I had heard at least a hundred times while traveling. I was on a plane, getting ready for it to take off, and we were going through the regular safety instructions: "In the case that there is a sudden drop in pressure in the main cabin, oxygen masks will drop…"

Most passengers, including myself, pay little attention to the instructions. But this time, for some unknown reason, I was paying careful attention. "Passengers are instructed to make sure their masks are on first before assisting other passengers or children."

This made me wonder, *Why? Why wouldn't I help others first before I attended to my own needs? Isn't that the selfless and caring thing to do?*

Well, it may be the selfless and caring thing to do, but it's not the smartest. If I try to help someone else get their mask on first, and I run out of oxygen, it won't do either of us any good!

This analogy pretty much sums up most people's experience with personal development. We are so busy taking care of other's needs—making project deadlines, being to meetings, running kids around, paying bills, making dinner, and so on and so on—that we run out of time for ourselves. Clearly, we also start "running out of oxygen" as we begin to burn out and become less valuable to those we are so busy trying to please.

Now, you might say, "Hold on a minute. You talked about the need to be selfless in Chapter One, to serve others, live the platinum rule, and put the team first. Now you are telling me to put myself first?" Indeed I am, as doing so relates to your own personal development. Putting others first is still important, but taking the time to develop yourself helps you improve not only your ability to be more selfless but also everything else we have talked about in this book.

When you focus on your own development, you become better. And you can't really be that good to anyone, including your team, if you aren't on top of your game and regularly learning and improving. So, develop yourself. It may require discipline; it won't always be convenient, and the effort might not seem worth it at times. But making your own self-development a priority is a critical investment with a guaranteed payoff.

Personal growth includes doing hard things. It's about attaining learning through knowledge, skills, and experience, and it is the best investment we can make. Benjamin Franklin once said, "For the best return on your money, pour your purse into your head."[11]

There is a direct correlation between the time you spend on your own growth and achieving personal greatness. Someone once shared a story with me that illustrates this point perfectly. It is the story of a grandson who would visit his grandfather's farm every year. One particular visit to the farm, the boy's grandfather was preparing to plant a few types of trees that he didn't already have on his farm. They both went to the local nursery to pick what trees they would plant.

When they got home, the warm, kind, loving, and wise grandfather asked his grandson, "If I plant one of these trees inside and plant one outside, which do you think will be the greatest?"

"I think the one inside will grow the biggest," answered the grandson, "because it won't have to deal with the cold winters, the wind, and the burning sun. It will face fewer hard things."

The grandfather took one of the trees and planted it indoors, and he planted the other outside. He turned to his grandson and said, "Let's see what happens."

For several years, the grandfather tended to both plants. It wasn't until the third year that the boy asked about the trees, having remembered the experiment. The old man took the boy to the tree they had planted outdoors and then to the tree they had planted indoors. "Which of the two trees do you think is greater?" asked the grandfather.

The boy answered, "The outside one, of course. But I don't know why. It had to deal with so much more than the tree inside."

"That is true," the grandfather said with a warm smile. "However, because the outside tree had to deal with so much more, it grew faster and became stronger. Do you think it was worth it?" asked the Grandfather.

"Definitely!" said the grandson, "Look at how its branches happily spread out to the sun and the sky."

The old wise man then taught his grandson something he would never forget. "Learning works the same way, my boy. If you choose to do nothing, you will grow very little and will begin to whither, just as this indoor tree has. If you choose to always take the path of least resistance, you will always be mediocre and average. You will only reach your full potential by purposely choosing to do the hard things, even when you don't feel like it—that's called discipline. This outdoor tree needed the hard things to become great."

With so many competing priorities, taking time for yourself can be difficult. But taking that time is the difference between being great and being average. One important self-development activity is reading. It is a great way to learn more about yourself and ways that you can become better. I personally love and subscribe to reading for growth, but it wasn't always that way. Reading has probably made the biggest difference in my professional life, and it can do the same for you. I really like the following quote that has been attributed to Fortune magazine, "Some people will lie, cheat, steal and back-stab to get ahead... and to think, all they have to do is READ."[12]

Did you know that if you read just a half a chapter a day (about 10-15 minutes) of an average non-fiction-length book, you could finish approximately 12 books in a year? Over a 10-year period, that would equate to 120 books; in 15 years, 180 books, and 240 books in 20 years! That's quite the library you could build, not to mention a phenomenal knowledge base! And it all happens just by reading 10-15 minutes a day.

In an article written by Tevi Troy in *Business Insider*, he states that former United States President George W. Bush read 186 books between 2006 and 2008 while serving as President. 14 were biographies on Abraham Lincoln alone. Compare this to the four books that the average American reads over the course of a year.[13] In fact, almost every president of the United States has been an avid reader. If the President of the United States can make time to read, it's hard to imagine any excuse we might have!

Another development activity is to participate in live or recorded webinars, online courses, teleconferences, or workshops. These days, there are unlimited opportunities with little to no cost to improve yourself. Did you know that many universities, including MIT, Harvard, and Cal Berkley, are offering hundreds of free online courses to the public? One site you can check for courses is www.edx.org.

It is important to highlight, however, that it isn't enough to simply read or attend a course or workshop. You must also take time to apply what you learn. You have probably had the experience, as most people have, of reading a book or attending an event with the intention of implementing some of the wonderful things that you have learned. But you never do because when you get back to your job and the day-to-day grind, your priorities shift.

I strongly encourage you to not let that happen. Learning requires a change in your behavior. You can read an entire book on living a virtuous life, but until you actually begin to live a virtuous life, you haven't really learned much. You can read an entire book on becoming a better teammate, but until you actually apply at least one or more of the principles you have read, you have learned very little.

The English Romantic poet John Keats once said in a letter to his older brother and sister-in-law, "Nothing ever becomes real till it is experienced - even a Proverb is no proverb to you till your Life has illustrated it."[14]

Closely related to the application of what you learn through reading, courses, and workshops is gaining experience. In the Wizard of Oz, the scarecrow asked, "Can't you give me brains?"

In response, the Wizard said, "A baby has brains, but it doesn't know much. Experience is the only thing that brings knowledge, and the longer you are on earth the more experience you are sure to get."[15]

A great deal of what we have learned in life is through experience, and the best way to gain experience on your team is to take on projects and assignments that stretch you. It is probably the quickest way for you to learn most things.

If you want to lead a project, reading and attending events will provide you a great knowledge base. But actually leading a project will provide you the quickest and the greatest value as you learn from your experience. If you want to sell widgets, reading and attending events will provide you a great foundation. But until you actually sell widgets, you won't amount to much of a sales person.

You can accelerate your career through taking on more experiences, especially those things outside of your comfort zone. Taking on difficult things will also quicken your personal growth.

Like the trees in the story above, if you do little, you will grow very little. Take the time each year to create a development plan that will move you towards your goals—then execute it. It won't always be easy, but I promise it will be worth it. Make it a priority.

Application: Are you taking adequate time to develop yourself? If not, why not? What are one or two things you can do now to work on your own personal development?

Inspire and Lead

As you work on yourself, others will naturally follow.

There is an old legend that tells of a French monastery that was well known throughout Europe because of the remarkable leadership of a man whom many called Brother Leo:

One year, a group of monks began the long journey to Brother Leo's monastery in hopes of learning from him. It was not long before the monks began arguing over who would carry out the various chores.

On the third day of their journey, they came across another monk who was going to visit Brother Leo, and he joined their party. This monk never murmured or shunned a duty. Whenever the other monks argued over a chore, he would humbly volunteer to do it himself. By the last day, the quarrelsome monks were following the example of this charitable monk, and everyone seemed to work together effortlessly.

When the traveling monks reached the monastery and asked for Brother Leo, their greeter laughed, saying, "But our brother is among you!" He pointed to the monk who had joined the traveling party late in the journey.[16]

In this story, Brother Leo demonstrates the power of example, and we can relate this old tale to the potential power YOU have to lead by example as well. Amazing things can happen when you take initiative and work to make the team better through your example. Being a leader is more about what you do than what you say or try to make others do.

Behind my house is a sidewalk that winds around the perimeter of a park. I have had the blessing of working from home for many years with a spectacular backdrop of this beautiful park and our colorful Southern Utah mountains. Almost without failure, as I look out my window every morning, I watch a tall, very elderly man make his way around the perimeter of the park at a slow but determined pace. Sometimes his wife joins him with her walker, and side-by-side in a slow, seasoned, and loving stride, they affectionately walk together.

This elderly man is a leader, and he doesn't even know it. He inspires me to not make excuses as to why I can't exercise today. He inspires me to not dread my sunset years. He inspires me as a husband to realize that lasting relationships are the golden dust of life. This quiet leader has had an important impact on me, and I don't even know him.

Who has inspired you and had an impact in your life? Was it a teacher? Maybe it was a spouse, friend, or teammate? My guess is that many people have had an impact on your life. Why? Because they were most likely doing something to improve themselves like my elderly friend. Perhaps they were trying to ease someone's burden, overcome an obstacle while remaining positive, or working hard to become something great. Whatever it was, when people try to do great things, they inspire with their desire to be better.

As you work on yourself, others will naturally follow. You don't have to be labeled as a team leader, manager, or boss to lead. If you have made the commitment to live the six *B's* in this book, you are taking the steps to lead and inspire others. You are also taking the steps to becoming a great teammate.

Application: What are you specifically doing on your team that inspires others? What other things can you do to inspire teammates? What kind of difference would it make?

Conclusion

Around 1100 AD, an unknown Monk wrote the following:

"When I was a young man, I wanted to change the world. I found it was difficult to change the world, so I tried to change my nation. When I found I couldn't change the nation, I began to focus on my town. I couldn't change the town and as an older man, I tried to change my family.

"Now, as an old man, I realize the only thing I can change is myself, and suddenly I realize that if long ago I had changed myself, I could have made an impact on my family. My family and I could have made an impact on our town. Their impact could have changed the nation and I could indeed have changed the world."[1]

You have a great opportunity to change others as you change yourself. Being a great teammate is as much about what you become, as it is about what you are doing to help others become. As you lead by example, others will follow.

As you work on becoming more selfless, trustworthy, humble, positive, respectful, and great, you are changing and improving your team. Just as I mentioned at the beginning of the book, great teams are made up of great teammates. But it starts with YOU. Your own success becomes everyone's success because that's how teams work!

My greatest wish is that something in this book has inspired you to be better. I hope with all of my heart that you will regularly think about the six *B's* and consistently work on improving each one of them. As you do so, your life will change. Not only will you become a greater teammate, but you will also become a greater person!

Michael G. Rogers

www.MichaelGRogers.com

What Kind of Teammate are You?

Use the scale below to indicate how each statement applies to your actions on the team. Reflect as completely and honestly as you can. Your responses and score will allow you to identify opportunities for improvement.

Take this assessment every few months to honestly reflect whether your behavior has changed. And remember, actions speak louder than words. As you take this assessment, ask others on your team for feedback.

If you have a copy of the Self-Study Workbook, you can complete this self-assessment here or in the workbook.

Scale:
3 = Most of the Time   2 = Some of the Time   1 = Rarely

1. Selfless

———— 1. I find opportunities to help and serve others on my team.

———— 2. I actively look for ways to help others on my team shine.

———— 3. I think about my teammates' needs.

———— 4. I put the team's needs ahead of my own aspirations and recognition.

2. Trustworthy

———— 5. I am always truthful (i.e., I don't stretch the truth, tell white lies, etc.).

_____ 6. I do what I say I will do.

_____ 7. I provide direct and sometimes difficult feedback to teammates as necessary.

_____ 8. I actively participate in team meetings. I provide my input, passionately discuss ideas, and challenge others.

3. Humble

_____ 9. I take personal accountability for my performance on the team.

_____ 10. I admit my mistakes to myself and others, and learn from them.

_____ 11. I seek feedback from others.

_____ 12. I implement the feedback I receive from others.

_____ 13. I take time to sincerely thank others on my team and those who provide support to my team.

4. Positive

_____ 14. I refrain from being negative on my team, including speaking negatively about my teammates.

_____ 15. I don't spread or participate in negative gossip on my team.

_____ 16. I take the time to genuinely and specifically compliment members of my team.

_____ 17. I positively encourage others on my team.

_____ 18. I actively look for ways to cheer and celebrate a teammate's success.

5. Respectful

_____ 19. I extend kindness to my teammates by regularly smiling; saying please, thank you, and you're welcome; actively listening; and saying and doing kind things.

_____ 20. I seek to truly understand a teammate before jumping to conclusions or becoming frustrated.

_____ 21. I am sincerely interested in the lives of my teammates.

_____ 22. I put myself in the shoes of my teammates as I try to understand them.

6. Great

_____ 23. I do more than what is required in my job.

_____ 24. I really understand and am passionate about my team's vision and goals.

_____ 25. I bring solutions, not problems, to my leader and team.

_____ 26. I invest time in my personal development.

_____ 27. I lead on my team by example.

_____ **TOTAL SCORE**

Scoring: The purpose of this assessment tool is to help you think and explore how you currently live the six virtues (*B's*) as a teammate. The assessment will provide you with a baseline, showing you where you can improve in living the six virtues through your actions. The ideal teammate will have only a few of these statements that are scored lower than a 3. However, few teammates are at the "ideal" teammate level, as it relates to the *6 B's*. But with work, you can get there.

_____ **Score of 77-81** indicates you are a strong teammate and have developed most or all of the six virtues (or *6 B's*).

_____ **Score of 72-76** indicates that while you can improve, you are doing better than most.

_____ **Score of 67-71** indicates that you have a balance of strengths and weaknesses with room to improve your practice in several of the virtues.

_____ **Score below 66** indicates an opportunity to improve upon most, if not all of the virtues.

Honestly answer each of the following five questions introspectively. They will help you to discover some important things around your role on the team, your effort, and commitment.

1. What is my personal contribution to the team? *This is not what you have the potential to contribute, but what you are actually contributing to the team today.*

_____

_____

_____

2. What is my contribution **potential** to the team? *What do you have the potential to bring that you aren't bringing today?*

_____

_____

_____

3. How committed am I to the team? What have I done to demonstrate my commitment?

_____

_____

_____

4. How would my teammates answer if they were asked questions one through three about me?

_____

_____

_____

5. What will I change based on my answers to the above questions?

_____

_____

_____

YOU ARE THE TEAM

BRING MICHAEL TO SPEAK AT YOUR NEXT EVENT

Michael is an Inc. Top 100 Leadership Expert Speaker

With over 20 years of experience in building leaders and teams, Michael is a great choice for keynotes and workshops.

"As a result of Mike's training I have developed dramatically as a leader. But more importantly my team is more effective and more unified as a result of the training." ~Eric Leavitt - CEO of the 10th largest Privately Held Insurance Brokerage in the US

www.MichaelGRogers.com/speaking

MichaelGRogers.com

109

YOU ARE THE TEAM E-COURSE

Can't get your team to a live event?

This course is a great substitute for Michael's *live* workshop.

Send your entire team through this self-paced interactive and engaging course. Concepts in the book are reinforced through a variety of activities.

www.MichaelGRogers.com/e-courses

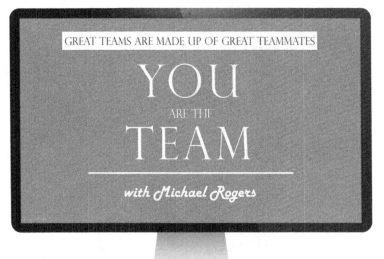

Bibliography

Chapter One: Be Selfless

1. Lisa Tendrich Frank, Editor, *The World of the Civil War [2 volumes]: A Daily Life Encyclopedia*, (Santa Barbara: ABC-CLIO,LLC, 2015), 425.
2. "The Price in Blood! Casualties in the Civil War," http://www.civilwarhome.com/casualties.htm.
3. Gilbert H. Muller, *Abraham Lincoln and William Cullen Bryant: Their Civil War,* (Port Washington: Palgrave MacMillan, 2017), 146.
4. History.com, "Battle of Fredericksburg," *History,* December 13, 2009, http://www.history.com/this-day-in-history/battle-of-fredericksburg.
5. Bill Dolack, "Heroism, Compassion, and Reconciliation by the Angel of Marye's Heights," *Christian History Society of America,* http://www.christianhistorysociety.com/kirkland.html.
6. David J. B. Trim, editor, *The Chivalric Ethos and the Development of Military Professionalism,* (Netherlands, Koninklijke Brill, 2003), 342.
7. Douglas K. Bassett, *Doctrinal Insights to the Book of Mormon, Volume III: Helaman through Moroni,* (Springville: Cedar Fort, Inc., 2008), 62.
8. Brian Cavanaugh, T.O.R., *The Sower's Seeds: 120 Inspiring Stories for Preaching, Teaching, and Public Speaking,* (Mahwah: Paulist Press, 2004), 30–31. Reprinted by permission.
9. Christine Comaford, "Yes You CAN Buy Happiness—And It's Cheaper Than You Think," *Forbes,* April 12, 2013, https://www.forbes.com/sites/christinecomaford/2013/04/12/yes-you-can-buy-happiness-and-its-cheaper-than-you-think/#168ac9e1c65b.

10. Jill Nystul, *One Good Life: My Tips, My Wisdom, My Story,* (New York: Penguin, 2015), 121.
11. "10 Ways to Cheer Yourself Up," http://www.homeremy.com/10-ways-to-cheer-yourself-up/.
12. "Virtue rewarded: Helping Others at Work Makes People Happier," *University of Wisconsin-Madison,* July 29, 2013, http://news.wisc.edu/virtue-rewarded-helping-others-at-work-makes-people-happier/.
13. Tony Alessandra and Michael J. O'Connor, *The Platinum Rule: Discover the Four Basic Business Personalities and How They Can Lead You To Success,* (New York: Warner Books, Inc., 1996).
14. Kevin Pritchard and John Eliot, Ph.D., *Help the Helper: Building a Culture of Extreme Teamwork,* (Kevin L. Pritchard and John F. Eliot, 2012), 51.
15. Stephanie Watson, "How to Improve Teamwork in the Workplace," *How Stuff Works,* http://money.howstuffworks.com/business/starting-a-job/how-to-improve-teamwork-in-workplace.htm.
16. Michael Rogers, "Working Together — Powerful Teamwork Story," *Teamwork and Leadership,* August 2012, http://www.teamworkandleadership.com/2012/08/work-together-powerful-teamwork-story.html.
17. "Harry S. Truman, 33rd President, 1945-1953," *Independent,* January 20, 2009, http://www.independent.co.uk/news/presidents/harry-s-truman-1451147.html.
18. Andre Bourque, "7 Leadership Lessons You Can Learn From the Game of Basketball," *Entrepreneur,* October 13, 2016, https://www.entrepreneur.com/article/273993.

Chapter Two: Be Trustworthy

1. Fred Shelley, *The World's Population: An Encyclopedia of Critical Issues, Crises, and Ever-Growing Countries,* (Santa Barbara: ABC-CLIO, 2015), 92.

2. Nate Scott, "Jack Sock Gives Point to Lleyton Hewitt in Incredible Moment of Sportsmanship," *USA Today Sports,* January 6, 2016, http://ftw.usatoday.com/2016/01/jack-sock-gives-point-to-lleyton-hewitt-in-incredible-moment-of-sportsmanship.

3. James E. Faust, "Honesty—A Moral Compass," *Ensign,* https://www.lds.org/general-conference/1996/10/honesty-a-moral-compass?lang=eng.

4. "10 Research Findings About Deception That Will Blow Your Mind," *Lie Spotting: Proven Techniques to Detect Deception,* June 10, 2010, http://liespotting.com/2010/06/10-research-findings-about-deception-that-will-blow-your-mind/.

5. Jerry Acuff, *Stop Acting Like a Seller And Start Thinking Like a Buyer: Improve Sales Effectiveness By Helping Customers Buy,* (New Jersey: John Wiley & Sons, Inc., 2007), 216.

6. Libby Plummer, "Little white lies are NOT as innocent as you think: Over time, small fibs may desensitize our brains to dishonesty," *DailyNews.com,* October 24, 2016, http://www.dailymail.co.uk/sciencetech/article-3860124/Little-white-lies-NOT-innocent-think-Small-fibs-slippery-slope-bigger-whoppers.html.

7. Gordon Leidner, "Lincoln's Honesty," *Great American History,* February 1999, http://www.greatamericanhistory.net/honesty.htm.

8. Curtis Hutson, *Great Preaching on Patriotism,* (United States: Sword of the Lord Publishers, 1988), 212.

9. Philip Elmer-DeWitt, "Steve Jobs: the Parable of the Stones," *Fortune,* November 11, 2011, http://fortune.com/2011/11/11/steve-jobs-the-parable-of-the-stones/.

10. Patrick Lencioni, *Five Dysfunctions of a Team,* (San Francisco: Jossey Bass, 2002), 202. Used by permission.

Chapter Three: Be Humble

1. Brian Cavanaugh, T.O.R., *More Sower's Seeds: Second Planting,* (Mahwah: Paulist Press, 1992), 47–48. Reprinted by permission.
2. Michael Rogers, "Meeting Participants Are Accountable, Too —3 Meeting Management Tips," *Teamwork and Leadership,* http://www.teamworkandleadership.com/2013/04/meeting-participants-are-accountable-too-3-meeting-management-tips.html.
3. Jack Canfield and Mark Victor Hansen, *A 2nd Helping of Chicken Soup for the Soul,* (Chicken Soup for the Soul Publishing, LLC. Published by Backlist, LLC, a unit of Chicken Soup for the Soul Publishing, LLC. Chicken Soup for the Soul is a registered trademark of Chicken Soup for the Soul Publishing, LLC. Reprinted by permission. All rights reserved. Copyright 2012).
4. Harvey Deutschendorf, "5 Ways to Reframe Your Failures," *Content Loop,* February 27, 2014, http://www.content-loop.com/5-ways-to-reframe-your-failures/.
5. Richard Farson and Ralph Keyes, *Whoever Makes the Most Mistakes Wins: A Paradox of Innovation,* (New York: The Free Press, 2002), 35.
6. Harry Beckwith, *Selling the Invisible: A Field Guide to Modern Marketing,* (New York: Warner Books, Inc., 1997).
7. Charlie Plumb, "'Parachute Packer' Story," *Captain J. Charles Plumb, http://speaker.charlieplumb.com/about-plumb/parachute-story/* Reprinted by permission.
8. Amy Morin, "7 Scientifically Proven Benefits of Gratitude That Will Motivate You To Give Thanks Year-Round," *Forbes,* November 23, 2014, https://www.forbes.com/sites/amymorin/2014/11/23/7-scientifically-proven-benefits-of-gratitude-that-will-motivate-you-to-give-thanks-year-round/#7be4089a183c.

Chapter Four: Be Positive

1. Michael Rogers, "Are You A Positive Leader? Great Story: 5 Rewards of Positive Leaders," *Teamwork and Leadership,*

October 2013,
http://www.teamworkandleadership.com/2013/10/are-you-a-positive-leader-great-story-5-rewards-of-positive-leaders.html.

2. Heryati R., "Habits of a Happy Employee at the Workplace,"
   6Q, https://inside.6q.io/habits-happy-employee-workplace/.

3. John Maxwell, *The 17 Indisputable Laws of Teamwork:
   Embrace Them and Empower Your Team,* (Nashville: Maxwell
   Motivation, Inc., 2001), 111. Reprinted by permission.

4. Ian Chadwick, "Great Minds, Small Minds," *Scripturient,* May
   30, 2015, http://ianchadwick.com/blog/great-minds-small-minds/.

5. Darren Poke, "The Triple Filter Test – A Story About Gossip,"
   Better Life Coaching Blog, September 10, 2010,
   https://betterlifecoachingblog.com/2010/09/10/the-triple-filter-test-a-story-about-gossip/.

6. Erin Schreiner, "When Can Gossip in the Workplace be
   Positive?" *The Nest,* http://woman.thenest.com/can-gossip-workplace-positive-10725.html.

7. "The Fable of the Deaf Frog – The Power of Words,"
   Academia Discover, January 28, 2015,
   https://academiadiscoverblog.wordpress.com/2015/01/28/the-fable-of-the-deaf-frog-the-power-of-words/.

8. Albert Bigelow Paine, *Mark Twain, a biography: the personal
   and literary life of Samuel Langhorne Clemens, volume IV*
   (New York: Harper & Brothers Publishers, 1912), 1334.

9. Michael Rogers, "Three Tips for Helping Employees Feel
   Valued," *Teamwork and Leadership,* May 2010,
   http://www.teamworkandleadership.com/2010/05/three-tips-for-helping-employees-feel-valued.html.

10. R. Mark Macy, "Why You Must Call "Time-Out" and
    Celebrate: Leadership Story," *Teamwork and Leadership,*
    November 2011,
    http://www.teamworkandleadership.com/2012/11/why-must-you-call-time-out-and-celebrate-leadership-story.html.
    Reprinted by permission.

11. Samuel Goldwyn quote: Ed McClements, "Financial – Sources
    of Funds During A Critical Illness," *LinkedIn,* January 25,

2016, https://www.linkedin.com/pulse/financial-sources-funds-during-critical-illness-ed.

Chapter Five: Be Respectful

1. "The Story of the Nails in the Fence," *The Lucky Penny,* May 8, 2012, https://luckypennylayne.com/2012/05/08/nails-in-the-fence/.
2. Doug Binder, "Prep Runner Carries Foe To Finish Line," June 5, 2012, http://www.espn.com/high-school/track-and-xc/story/_/id/8010251/high-school-runner-carries-fallen-opponent-finish-line.
3. Kara Deschenes, "The Kindness of Runners," *Women's Running,* June 27, 2012, http://womensrunning.competitor.com/2012/06/inspiration/the-kindness-of-runners_2652#ozbutMOwccyhd47E.97.
4. Prem, "Best Quotes by Mother Teresa Will Surely Boost the Spirit of Humanity," *TF Live,* August 25, 2016, http://techfactslive.com/mother-teresa-birthday-inspirational-quotes/7090/.
5. Gayle LaSalle, "Be a Grateful Leader – Thank You and You're Welcome Goes a Long Way!" *Teamwork and Leadership,* August 2012, http://www.teamworkandleadership.com/2012/08/be-a-grateful-leader-thank-you-and-youre-welcome-goes-a-long-ways.html. Reprinted by permission.
6. Bob Bourgault, "Kindness," *Almond Acres Charter Academy,* December 6, 2016, http://www.aacacademy.com/single-post/2016/12/06/Kindness.
7. Amanda Redhead, "Parenting and the Simple Power of Touch," *The Huffington Post,* March 10, 2016, http://www.huffingtonpost.com/amanda-redhead/parenting-and-the-simple-power-of-touch_b_9366616.html.
8. Ryunkandl, "Dog Legends: Gelert of Wales," *imgur,* April 4, http://imgur.com/gallery/ucevRR7.
9. Sarah Gibson, "Here's Why You Should Be Kind To Everyone, Always," *Collective Evolution,* March 22, 2015,

http://www.collective-evolution.com/2015/03/22/heres-why-you-should-be-kind-to-everyone-always/.

10. Cleveland Clinic, "Empathy: the Human Connection to Patient Care." YouTube video, 4:23. Posted February 2013. https://www.youtube.com/watch?v=cDDWvj_q-o8.

11. Amish proverb: "Value of the Month: Empathy," March 1, 2017, http://colegioliceosorolla.es/valor-del-mes-empatia/.

Chapter Six: Be Great

1. M. Russell Ballard, "Finding Joy Through Loving Service," *Ensign*, May 2011, 46. Reprinted by permission.

2. Corinne J. Naden and Rose Blue, *African American Biographies: Wilma Rudolph,* (Chicago: Raintree, 2004), 7.

3. Eric Garner, "You Have to Want It," *Evancarmichael.com*, http://www.evancarmichael.com/library/eric-garner/You-Have-To-Want-To.html.

4. Stacy Pettinelli Mulligan, "What's Holding You Back From Your Goals?" *Tailored For You Fitness,* July 24, 2015, http://tailoredforyoufitness.com/holding-you-back-from-your-goals/.

5. "1954, Roger Bannister Breaks 4-Minutes Mile," *History,* http://www.history.com/this-day-in-history/roger-bannister-breaks-four-minutes-mile.

6. MWG, *Quiet Moment with God Devotional Journal for Women,* (Colorado Springs: Honor Books, 2003), 92.

7. "Aesop's Belling the Cat Fable," *Agify.me,* March 2015, http://www.agify.me/wp-content/uploads/2015/03/The-Teamwork-Oscars-Aesops-Belling-the-Cat-Fable.pdf.

8. Monroe Mann, "Battle Cries for the Underdog: Fightin' words for an extrodinary life, volume 1, (Bloomington: AuthorHouse, 2006), 104.

9. Robert D. McFadden, "Nicholas Winton, Rescuer of 669 Children From Holocaust, Dies at 106," *New York Times,* July 1, 2015, https://www.nytimes.com/2015/07/02/world/europe/nicholas-

winton-is-dead-at-106-saved-children-from-the-holocaust.html?_r=0.

10. Robert D. McFadden, "Nicholas Winton, Rescuer of 669 Children From Holocaust, Dies at 106," *New York Times,* July 1, 2015, https://www.nytimes.com/2015/07/02/world/europe/nicholas-winton-is-dead-at-106-saved-children-from-the-holocaust.html?_r=0.

11. Myrko Thum, "Why Personal Development is the Best Investment You'll Ever Make," *Myrko Thum,* September 15, 2013, http://www.myrkothum.com/best-investment/.

12. Sabrina Peterson, "7 Business Books that Every Entrepreneur Should Read," *Rolling Out,* September 2, 2016, http://rollingout.com/2016/09/02/7-business-books-entrepreneur-read/.

13. Tevi Troy, "8 Fascinating Stories About Presidents and Their Favorite Books," *Business Insider,* February 17, 2014, http://www.businessinsider.com/8-surprising-tales-of-presidential-reading-2014-2.

14. John Keats, edited by H. Buxton Forman, *The Complete Works of John Keats, Vol. V, Letters 1819 and 1820,* (Glasgow: Gowards & Gray, 1901), 38.

15. L. Frank Baum, *The Wonderful Wizard of Oz,* (Chicago: Harper Trophy, 1987), 223.

16. Michael Josephson, "Commentary: The Parable of Brother Leo," *What Will Matter,* July 15, 2016, http://whatwillmatter.com/2016/07/commentary-835-4-the-parable-of-brother-leo/amp/. Reprinted by permission.

Conclusion

1. Larry Chang, *Wisdom for the Soul: Five Millennia of Prescriptions for Spiritual Healing,* (Washington, DC: Gnosophia Publishers, 2006), 111.